CURTAINS and

HISTORY · DESIGN · INSPIRATION

DRAPERIES

CURTAINS and

HISTORY · DESIGN · INSPIRATION

DRAPERIES

JENNY GIBBS

The Overlook Press
Woodstock · New York

First published in 1994 by
The Overlook Press
Lewis Hollow Road
Woodstock, New York 12498

First published in the UK 1994 by Cassell, London

Library of Congress Cataloging-in-Publication Data

Gibbs, Jenny.
Curtains and draperies : history, design, inspiration / Jenny Gibbs.
p. cm.
1. Drapery – Europe – History.   2. Drapery – United States – History.
3. Drapery in interior decoration. I. Title.

NK3242.G53   1994   93-40333
747'.3 – dc20   CIP

ISBN 0-87951-539-2

Typeset by Litho Link Limited, Welshpool, Powys.
Printed and bound in Slovenia by Mladinska Knjiga
by arrangement with Korotan Italiana

Second printing

Contents

Introduction

Curtains and drapes are undergoing something of a renaissance today, with the past providing a rich source of inspiration. Many elements in a room combine to create a particular ambience, but the curtain treatment is one of the most eye-catching and therefore crucial to get right. An integral part of the interior design, it can, in fact, be the keynote of the whole room. Hanging and draped fabrics need not be restricted to the windows, of course – the drapery on beds, in doorways, even on walls and ceilings also offers enormous creative potential. Nor do window treatments have to be limited to curtains: various forms of drapery, as well as a variety of attractive blinds, can work equally well.

The styles of the past seem to hold more of a fascination than ever, and increasing numbers of people are seeking to create authentic period interiors. Many are concerned to achieve authenticity in every detail, and this approach is, of course, completely appropriate in some instances. With curtains and drapery, as with other furnishings, faithfully reproduced historic treatments can produce splendid effects which complement the architecture and furniture perfectly.

Even in a period home, however, a style that suits the people living there and their way of life is a priority. Indeed, creative mixing of styles can sometimes work just as well as a more purist approach in a period house. Where historical accuracy is not essential, it is simply a delight to take inspiration from a period window treatment and adapt its details. The result in a modern interior, for example, can be fresh, original and sympathetic to the architecture of the building. Period styles of decoration, and in particular of curtains and drapery, can be adapted to a variety of settings, and past and present can be effectively combined, creating a home with character and originality.

INFORMED INSPIRATION

Nevertheless, to avoid achieving what amounts to a visual ragbag, you need imagination, ingenuity – and a good working knowledge of historic styles. Successful adaptations depend on this just as much as authentic reproductions do. Skilful interpretations and truly inspired innovations cannot be done in a vacuum; they must be based on a firm foundation of background knowledge. Armed with this, you should be able to achieve anything from a flavour of the past to a fully fledged, completely authentic historic treatment.

One of the most interesting changes I have noticed since setting up the KLC School of Interior Design in London in 1982 is that the approach of the students has gradually become less superficial. As far as curtains and drapes are concerned, they like to know why a particular window or bed treatment evolved and what the accompanying interior would have been like, as a background to devising an appropriate treatment.

I believe that this is, in fact, the only way to understand period styles of curtains and drapes or, for that matter, interior design. Once the background and influences that led to particular styles are known, the treatments can be seen in their original context, which will inspire a greater, more appropriate range of ideas.

USING THIS BOOK

The book is divided into chapters covering broad headings of recognized style periods. While developments in style do not always obligingly fit into these specific periods, they are fairly representative of the prevailing fashions and attitudes. Each chapter begins with a historical overview, building up a general picture of the era. It sets out the key features of the style and analyses the underlying influences, such as political upheavals and war, attitudes of the court and fashions among the gentry, and the leading architects and designers. This is followed by a section on the lifestyle of the time, as it was reflected inside the homes – how they were lived in and what the rooms actually looked like.

After this, the focus is on various aspects of the curtains and drapes themselves. This section, the heart of the book, also examines the development of windows, beds and their hangings, fabrics and trimmings. A recurring theme running through all the text is the influence the Continent, Britain and America have continually had on each other's interior decoration. The final chapter analyses the whole subject from a different angle, discussing the factors to consider when deciding on window treatments and fabrics; suitable historical treatments are suggested for all the principal types of window.

The illustrations too are a mixture of pure historical treatments and modern interpretations, to help you adapt period ideas for curtains and drapes to the requirements of modern living. I hope the book will help you find as much enjoyment and inspiration in the subject as I have.

1

THE 15TH & 16TH CENTURIES

The Renaissance

The Renaissance marked a turning away from the Gothic styles of the medieval period and a return to Classical, especially Roman, architectural forms and principles. On a broader scale, it reflected a new sense of optimism, a belief in human genius, a reawakening or rebirth, after the Dark Ages. The Renaissance first flowered in Florence and other prosperous Italian cities early in the 15th century, reaching its peak there around 1500–1520, and it spread throughout Italy and much of Western Europe, including England, during the 16th century.

Before then, medieval homes, with their ground plan that was very basic and their lack of privacy, had been distinctly lacking in comfort by modern standards. Simple dwellings had consisted of little more than four walls and a roof, and most activities such as cooking and housework had taken place outdoors. Larger houses usually had one great hall, which had a central fireplace and which was where the family cooked, ate and slept. In short, medieval homes had been little more than a crude shelter, with defence and security more of a priority than decoration. Windows with glass had been rare in medieval times; paper, horn or wooden shutters had been used to keep out the cold. Textiles had not featured much in medieval homes. They were incredibly expensive, and importation costs put them beyond the reach of any but the most wealthy households. This is the main reason they were one of the later forms of decoration, particularly in England, which was well behind Italy and France in textile production. And even when textiles did start to feature in interiors, during the Renaissance, they became bed and wall hangings before they were ever used as any form of window drapery.

The walls and bed are richly draped in this late 14th century French interior, but at the windows removable shutters keep out the light and cold. Although the upper windows and the shutters are glazed here, glass was rare at this time.

INFLUENCES

It was really with the Renaissance that an identifiable style of decoration began to emerge in England and continental Europe. There was a new awareness of interior decoration, and inspiration was taken

9

Typical Renaissance-style ornament with entwining scroll and acanthus motifs, caryatids (pillars in the form of draped female figures), putti (cherubs) and cornucopias.

from the Classical civilizations. Architecture and interiors began to feature the Classical orders and decorative motifs such as grotesques, garlands, lion masks, cupids, cornucopias and arabesques.

Italy was at the forefront of this movement. There, as a result of private patronage, decoration became as important in the home as it had traditionally been in the Church. There was a new symmetry and harmony in architecture; and interiors, which were highly decorated with wood carving, painted panels, ornate plasterwork and frescoes, were elegant and perfectly proportioned.

The skills of Italian craftsmen were brought into France in 1483, when Charles VIII of France annexed most of Italy and brought back a number of Italian artists and craftsmen to the French court. By the beginning of the 16th century, however, the Italians were in some decline as leaders of taste, and the French were in the ascendancy. Although the Italian nobles were passionate about the construction and decoration of splendid villas, the prolonged years of war with France had drastically reduced the amount of money available.

In 1515 Francis I of France commissioned a project of huge significance to the development of interior decoration, namely the interior of Fontainebleau. The style was really a French interpretation of Italian Renaissance, and French, Italian and Flemish craftsmen were brought in to work on it. The great ground-floor gallery of the New Wing of the Louvre museum is another good example of the French Renaissance style.

English interior style began to change, but only very gradually. This was partly due to Henry VIII's quarrel with the Pope, which left England very isolated. Henry had incurred the Pope's wrath when, despite failing to gain Papal authorization to have his marriage to Catherine of Aragon nullified, he married his new love, Anne Boleyn, and then appointed himself head of the Church of England into the bargain. This turn of events, combined with the sheer geographical distances, meant that the Italian writings and pattern books that were influencing much of the rest of Europe reached England much later. (The invention of printing by William Caxton had, however, made books more available and affordable and had begun the process of the nation becoming better-informed.) English Renaissance style was rather piecemeal, incorporating some continental European ideas but never really embracing the style as a satisfactory whole. It produced some fine but often disjointed decoration. Renaissance country houses such as Longleat, the earliest surviving example of English Renaissance architecture, and Wollaton Hall, near Nottingham, captured some of the grand and spacious spirit of the movement but remained highly individual.

With textiles now beginning to play a part in interiors, it is the perfect point for the purposes of this book to take up the story.

Inspiration for interior draperies often came from military camps, as in this mid 15th century striped tented bed canopy suspended from the ceiling.

LIFESTYLE

In the 15th century, large households were still very mobile. Even the bed, which was by far the most important piece of furniture at this time, was demountable. Life centred around the great hall, which sometimes had a raised dais at one end used by the most high-ranking members of the household. Before the family arrived, the house would be transformed by hangings, which were used both for decoration and to reduce draughts. Fine hangings divided the hall into more intimate areas. These were suspended by rings on rods attached to columns or the wall. Other hangings were draped around the bed and over benches to soften the seating. Tables were covered with fabric and swagged. On festive occasions the dais and balconies would be hung with banners and standards. In fine weather draperies would be set up in the garden; again the tables and benches would be draped in fabric, and also garlanded with flowers.

In England the end of the Wars of the Roses in the late 15th century brought a greater permanence to homes, in keeping with the more stable state of the country. The marriage of Henry VII of York to Elizabeth of Lancaster marked a new period of security and prosperity, which allowed the decorative arts to flourish, though they sometimes lacked the restraint and refinement of their European counterparts.

Beds were no longer transported from one establishment to another, and wall hangings were often seamed together to fit a particular room. These hangings must have been very beautiful, with their rich borders, and their seams cleverly disguised with strips of silk or metal lace.

The layout of the house was evolving, with the great hall now galleried. The gallery became a feature of 16th century houses and was used for displaying treasures and for exercise and conversation. While the great hall had been the hub of the household's life in the early 15th century, its importance gradually declined, so that by the end of the 16th century it was simply used as a servants' hall and an entrance hall. The great chamber, upstairs, had become the most important ceremonial room and was often as large as the hall. A withdrawing chamber usually adjoined the great chamber, and this gradually began to be used as a private sitting, eating and reception room. Beyond that was a bedchamber and the gallery. Downstairs, one or more parlours served as intimate sitting and eating rooms.

Wood panelling, early hand-blocked wallpapers and embossed leather were alternatives to wall hangings and tapestries in wealthy homes, while modest homes had painted cloth hangings on the walls. In richer homes, woven and needlework carpets were used on the floors, while rush matting sufficed in simpler homes. Oriental rugs were certainly imported, but evidence suggests that that they were draped over tables rather than being used on the floor.

Carved oak beams and decorative plasterwork were features of the period, while the lavish use of motifs and ornament was a sign of the influence of master-plasterers first from Italy and then from Holland and Germany. Until the second half of the 16th century, England had tended to ally itself socially with France and Italy. But under Elizabeth I – who, like her father Henry VIII, was a Protestant and kept England under Protestant rule – the country found itself more naturally allied politically and socially with the Low Countries and Germany. This influence translated itself into the interiors of the Elizabethan period. Whereas the Italian-inspired early 16th century decoration featured arabesques, medallion heads and cupids, the Dutch and German influence showed itself in the strapwork and patterns in plasterwork

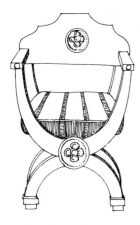

The X-frame chair was commonly found in many countries during medieval and Renaissance times.

and the style of panelling and furniture that developed in the mid to late 16th century. It became fashionable for wealthy landowners to travel to Holland and Flanders, as well as to France, in order to gather ideas for their houses.

Furniture and Upholstery

Seating was fairly basic at this time. Stools, the most common form of seating in the 16th century, developed into joined stools, which were put together by a joiner using proper joints. There were very few chairs before the 17th century, but the earliest ones were panelled and carved, with wooden seats. It was often the practice to place outsize cushions on the floor for the ladies to sit on and to protect them from

Tapestries and other forms of wall hanging were one of the main forms of decoration in early interiors. Here a fine tapestry against linenfold panelling provides a splendid backdrop to Tudor furniture.

A magnificent yellow bed in the King's Room, Traquair House, Scotland. Recently restored, it was said to have been used by Mary, Queen of Scots. The coverlet is attributed to her workmanship.

the rush matting. Until 1600 the usual way to make a seat comfortable was to put a cushion on it; upholstery did not exist. Indeed, real comfort as we know it was not a priority in Renaissance interiors. These cushions, however, played an important part in the overall decoration, with damask and velvet being favourite fabrics. It was quite usual in wealthy houses of the period for the chairs to be draped or cushioned in heavily embroidered material that matched the bed hangings. Henry VIII's possessions included a chair of turned wood painted walnut colour, with the seat and back covered in black velvet embroidered with Venice gold and fringed with yellow and black silks.

Other furniture found in affluent homes of the time included a refectory table surrounded by chairs and stools, trestle tables (used by the servants and then dismantled after each meal), court cupboards and smaller cupboards, chests and clothes presses. The settle first appeared in the 16th century, and chairs included back stools, box chairs and X-frame chairs. Furniture was made mainly of oak. In the late 16th century, inlaid furniture became fashionable.

Colours

The homes of the 15th and 16th centuries relied heavily on colour and textiles to make them cheerful and welcoming. Interior walls were often painted in strong colours and patterns, and the whole effect would have been vibrant and welcoming. In houses of this period still surviving today, there is little evidence of the once brightly coloured walls, and the draperies have disintegrated long ago. It is thus hard to picture just how attractive these barren halls could be made.

The natural dyes of the time provided jewel-like colours reminiscent of the magnificently illustrated medieval manuscripts. Wealthy homes were full of rich and vivid colours like earthy reds, deep and light greens (particularly fashionable), lemon yellow and deep blues such as lapis lazuli, set off by silver and gold. Around the middle of the 16th century a vogue developed for deep colours like rich violet, midnight blue and dark green, again with gold or silver trimmings. (In humbler homes, however, where these rare and expensive dyes were unaffordable, the palette was restricted to earth pigments and was therefore considerably more subdued.)

CURTAINS AND DRAPERY

Although window curtains, as such, did not exist in England until the late 16th century, forms of drapery were used to partition off parts of the great hall for privacy, and to provide canopies and curtains for the bed. Wall hangings were a popular form of decoration.

Curtains over doors were more common than window curtains in the 16th century and were often in tapestry to match the wall hangings. In all types of curtain, France and Italy were more advanced than England.

Beds and Bed Hangings

The bed was by far the most expensive piece of furniture in a household of this period – it was a symbol of the wealth and importance of its owner. The bedstead itself was usually low and the earliest draperies were held up on rods stretched across the room by means of cords attached to hooks in the ceiling. This later evolved into a canopy or tester which was supported by a headboard and corner posts. These corner posts were often rather bulbous in shape due to the lathe turning and were carved ornately.

The bed curtains were usually made of tapestry, rich silk velvet or brocatelle (a type of silk strengthened with linen). Probably imported from Arabia or Italy, they would have been very expensive. When not in use during the day, the curtains were gathered into bags suspended at the corners. Not only were the actual bed hangings rich but the bed would have been generously supplied with linen and pillows, blankets and cushions.

The lavish costumes of the day echoed the richly decorated interiors, and clothing was opulently embroidered in gold or silver threads, an effect which was later much used on furnishing textiles.

In France bed drapery became relatively sophisticated in the 16th century, much of it inspired by antique drapery in churches and temples. The valances were shaped, fringed, tasselled and ornamented. The suspended canopy was sometimes replaced by a solid four-poster bed with a wooden canopy, the posts heavily carved. The draperies were incredibly rich with, for example, gold designs on black velvet, or green and white motifs on red velvet. Queen Catherine of Medici had a magnificent bed in black velvet decorated with pearls.

Windows

In the Middle Ages, windows had been small and narrow for defensive purposes and probably covered with nothing more than oiled or waxed paper. Although there was some form of glazing as early as

A reconstruction of a medieval bed set on a covered platform and draped in monogrammed silk. To suit the wealthy owner's peripatetic lifestyle, the bed could be dismantled and moved around from house to house. During the day the curtains were put into the bag suspended from the canopy.

the 13th or 14th century, it only became standard in larger farmhouses and town houses from the late 16th century and was not in general use for another hundred years.

A simple window in the 16th century would have been an unglazed square opening divided by a series of stone or wooden mullions. Protection from the elements came from internal wooden shutters. By the end of the century horizontal bars were standard and the small panes were often diamond-shaped. In homes where there was no glass the wicker or oak lattice frame would be filled with cloth, paper or occasionally horn. Sometimes parchment was stretched across a lattice frame and decorated with figurative patterns or coats of arms, before being oiled. The criss-cross pattern of the leaded diamonds in the first

glazed windows echoed these lattices. Throughout England and Europe windows increased in size as glass became more readily available and the quality improved.

Charming coronetted hangings in the Queen's Bathroom at Leeds Castle. The washing tub, table and stool are also draped in fabric.

Curtains

In England, shutters were used to keep out light and cold, and curtains were virtually non-existent until well into the 16th century. The earliest forms of curtaining were drawn from one side of the window only. Made from one piece of material, the curtain was hung on an iron rod, suspended from iron rings sewn directly onto the fabric itself or by fabric tapes sewn on in the same way.

These metal curtain hooks
sewn onto a curtain and
hooked over a pole are similar
to those used in the 16th
century.

Right: An early method of
suspension, with metal rings
sewn directly onto the curtain.
These were then slotted onto a
metal pole with a hooked end
to prevent the curtains from
sliding off.

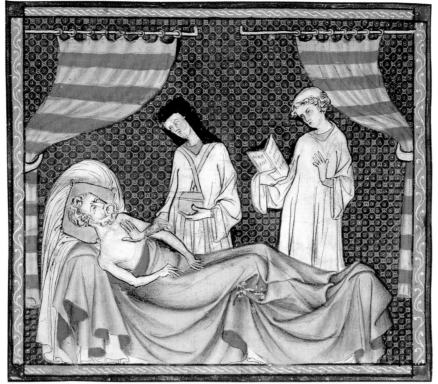

Opposite: In this modern
room a single curtain caught
back over French windows is
hung in the early style with the
top of the curtain forming
wide loops, which hang from a
simple pole.

French and Italian curtains of the time were more elaborate. Made
from velvet or brocade, they were hung in pairs but were fairly narrow
and did not reach the floor.

In the 16th century, military camps were often a source of
inspiration for interiors. One such model was the camp *"du drap d'or"*
erected by Francis I for the reception of Henry VIII in 1520, with
richly coloured standards and drapery shot with gold.

In France in the latter half of the 16th century curtains were used as
draught excluders at doorways, where they were known as portières;
here and on the beds they were often combined with shaped pelmets
quite richly ornamented with embroidered appliqué.

Fabrics

Marvellous fabrics were being produced by ancient civilizations for
many centuries before the Renaissance. The ancient Egyptians' woven
textiles, for example, were imported by the Greeks and Romans. The
Chinese invented silk weaving around four thousand years ago and
produced nearly all the world's silk for centuries. By the 14th century the
Italian weavers of Lucca and Florence were producing exquisite figured
silk velvets. These were often designed for specific purposes such as
upholstery or wall hangings. In the 15th century the Italians found
themselves competing with the newly developed French industry.

By the beginning of the Renaissance, symmetrical patterns had been
replaced with asymmetry and there was more movement in the

Simple portière curtains caught back in a pair of arched doorways make a suitable decorative feature in a period house.

designs, with floral scrolls, birds in flight or running animals. (Interestingly, although it is not surprising to find many examples of the influence of architecture on the decorative arts and fabric design, the fact that throughout the history of art there have also been numerous examples of architectural ornament being inspired by decorative fabrics or embroidery is more surprising. The Renaissance is one such time.) Until the 16th century most patterns woven into silks were large, but from around that time the use to which the fabric would be put was taken into account. Silks to be used for upholstery would often have smaller patterns than those destined for walls.

Damask, first produced in Europe in the late 15th century, was a favourite material of the period. It takes its name from Damascus, the capital of Syria, which was an important centre of the silk trade. Although traditionally made of silk or linen, damask can be woven in wool or a mix of fibres. The fluid yet formal patterns created by the contrast between the matt sateen-weave motifs and the glossy satin-weave ground have remained unchanged through the centuries and are still instantly recognizable today.

In the 15th century, Bruges was the most important Northern European port trading with Italy. It was also where the Flemish linen-thread weavers worked, and linen damask evolved as these Flemish craftsmen copied the patterns of the Italian silk damask in their own linen thread. By the early 16th century they had developed their own designs. Early velvets came mainly from Genoa in Italy. Also at this time Italian and Flemish weavers were established at Fontainebleau to produce tapestries and at Lyons to weave silk.

Silk was woven in England from the early 1400s. Medieval fabrics included a wide range of silk-based fabrics with exotic names such as holosericum, subsericum, examitum or cendal. Camak or camoca, used for the drapery of state beds, was made of silk mixed with camel hair. Only the wealthiest households could afford silk, so wool or linen was more commonly used.

Towards the end of the 16th century, the first *indiennes* – brightly coloured hand-blocked and hand-painted calicoes that were colourfast, unlike the crude European prints – were introduced into France from India. They were imported mainly through the port of Marseilles and immediately proved very popular. Throughout the 15th and 16th centuries, as dyeing techniques spread to the West from the East, the colouring of fabrics advanced and improved, although European block-printing techniques remained crude for some time.

Trimmings

The Italians were the first masters of beautiful hand-sewn trimmings. As Italian craftsmen became established in France, this type of work was also seen there and in England. Ropes and tassels in a variety of shapes and sizes were used to hold back bed curtains and give definition to early pelmets on beds and portières. These pelmets were often ornamented with embroidery appliquéd onto the surface. Lace was also used as an edging for pelmets and early curtains.

This pair of portières held back with ropes and tassels and surmounted by a pelmet decorated with appliquéd embroidery is typical of a 16th century doorway treatment.

A 16th century Italian textile showing the influence of the elaborate interwoven strapwork motifs of the Renaissance.

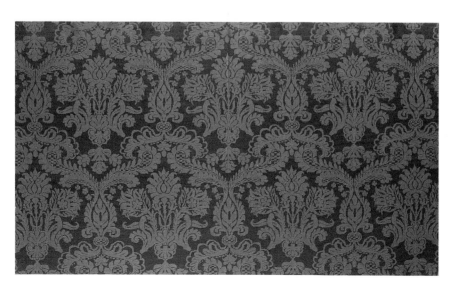

2

THE 17TH CENTURY
The Baroque

By the early 17th century, the Classicism of the Renaissance was evolving in Italy into the theatrical and ornate Baroque style, which spread from Italy around Europe during the 17th century, reaching England around the 1670s. Though often very grand, even grandiose, it formed the basis for modern ideas of interior decoration.

In the first few decades of the 1600s, comfort was still not a priority. Interiors were designed as a background to social gatherings, they were status symbols and little consideration was given to comfort. An innovation of the Baroque style was that suites of furniture, together with mirrors and paintings, were specifically designed as an integral part of the scheme. For the first time, important painters of the time created works for domestic as well as ecclesiastical interiors.

Italian Baroque interiors featured wonderful plasterwork, which gave flat surfaces a three-dimensional effect, giving the impression of there being no visible division between walls and ceilings, and decoration such as wreaths or cornucopias superimposed on the interior architecture. The buildings themselves were characterized by large-scale planning, theatricality, bold curving lines and an adventurous treatment of Classical elements.

INFLUENCES

Until this time, the French and the English had had few architects. Major projects had often been undertaken by specialist craftsmen working from engravings of the work of Italian architects. In France this now changed. At the beginning of the 17th century, Henry IV encouraged craftsmen by putting them under royal protection. His successor, Louis XIII, fostered a national style, and then in the middle of the century Louis XIV commissioned wonderful work at Versailles from such architects as François Mansart, Louis Le Vau and Charles Le Brun. Le Brun was really the first all-round interior decorator and architect. He took Le Vau's rooms at Versailles and transformed them

Although this scene was painted early in the 18th century, the style of the room remains inherently Baroque, with the rich, two-tone green hangings, silver chandelier and lacquer cabinet.

23

into something of real brilliance. The style, which was widely imitated, was typified by rich, sombre colours, mirrors, marble, the use of wood on floors and walls, velvet wall coverings and themed tapestries with gold and silver thread.

There were, of course, many Italian artists already established in France, as Charles VIII had brought them back on his return from the Naples campaign. Indeed, the Italians' frescoes, *trompe l'oeil*, *faux* finishes, gildings, sculpture and furniture appeared all over Europe as they fulfilled commissions. Nevertheless, the French increasingly produced more of a national style. There was a return to the Classical orders, and the Louis XIV style of decoration is usually considered to be architecturally inspired. Private building proliferated in Paris, much of it commissioned by the middle classes as well as the aristocracy.

After 30 years of war with Spain, Germany was on the road to recovery, and craftsmen were greatly encouraged in special court workshops. The Spanish, though a dwindling power at this stage, greatly impoverished by the lengthy war, still managed to keep their arts and architecture flourishing. The Netherlands, freed from Spanish domination, developed as an important sea power and achieved great colonial wealth. Their most influential architect was Hans Vredeman de Vries, and their greatest contribution was to the intimate, small-scale type of interior rather than larger, grander projects, which were not always so successful.

For England the 17th century was a time of great change. Elizabeth I had died without leaving an heir, so James VI of Scotland – son of Mary, Queen of Scots – came to the throne as James I of England, proclaiming himself "King of Great Britain". He encouraged links with the Continent, and so it was during the Jacobean period (James ruled from 1603 till 1625) that the first real understanding of design in architecture and interior decoration emerged in England.

James I was succeeded by his son, Charles I, whose high-handed and inflexible approach brought him into direct conflict with Parliament. This finally led to civil war between the Cavaliers (for the King and his lords) and the Roundheads (for Parliament and the people). The King was captured and beheaded in 1649, and his son, Charles, fled to France. Cromwell, the leader of the Roundheads, ruled competently for some years, but the Commonwealth was a stagnant time for art and design. When Cromwell's son was unable to succeed him satisfactorily, the people yearned again for the excitement and style of the monarchy, and in 1660 the Stuarts were restored to the throne in the person of Charles II. He was succeeded by James II and then William and Mary of Orange.

The major influence on the architectural styles of the period was the architect and stage designer Inigo Jones, regarded as the founder of English Classical architecture. He learned his draughting skills in Italy and developed a deep admiration for the Classical architecture he saw

A lavish portière curtain caught back in the arched doorway of a 17th century Dutch home. Intimate, small-scale interiors like this were a feature of the Netherlands' interpretation of the Baroque.

and studied there, particularly that of the 16th century Venetian architect Andrea Palladio. It was Jones who first introduced the Palladian style to England. From 1615 until the middle of the century Jones worked on a number of notable commissions, such as the Queen's House at Greenwich (the country's first Palladian mansion) and the Banqueting House in Whitehall, through his post as Surveyor of the King's Works. The work he carried out in the 1650s at Wilton House, in Wiltshire, was a perfect example of his Palladian style. Inigo Jones was a man ahead of his time, however. His precepts had little impact outside of court circles until after the Restoration, and it wasn't until the early part of the next century that his genius was fully appreciated.

The Restoration brought the return of the English aristocracy from the courts of Holland and France, and they favoured the continental Baroque style. They came back to a country where hygiene was appalling, and the Plague spread like wildfire, with disastrous results not only for life but also for trade. In 1666 there was also the Great Fire; this almost demolished the City of London and further depleted the country's timber stocks, which were already so low that legislation had been introduced to protect them.

A great deal of building and rebuilding followed the Great Fire. Sweden supplied much of the timber for this, prompting trade between the two countries. One of the chief architects of this time was Sir Christopher Wren, whose town houses became a blueprint for the future. He was so impressed by the high standard of French workmanship he had seen in Paris that he trained craftsmen specially for the decoration of royal palaces, St. Paul's Cathedral and churches in the City of London. As well as St. Paul's Cathedral and over 50 Baroque churches, he designed a number of other buildings, including the Royal Exchange, Greenwich Observatory and Trinity College, Cambridge. He also partly rebuilt Hampton Court Palace, which was heavily influenced by the palace of Versailles. Many of Wren's buildings have remained landmarks of lasting beauty.

While Sir Christopher Wren had originally been a professor of astronomy before turning to architecture, his contemporary, Sir John Vanbrugh, was a successful playwright as well as an architect. With the ultimate in English Baroque buildings – Castle Howard and Blenheim Palace – to his credit, Vanbrugh was the architect most responsible for creating the English Baroque style.

Despite the enthusiasm with which it was embraced, private patronage of the English Baroque style was not always entirely successful. In particular, where attempts were made to create hugely grand and impressive interiors, the style somehow seems out of sympathy with British taste.

In the eastern American colonies, established in the early part of the century, the architecture showed signs of Dutch Baroque, with some

German and Scandinavian influence, though there were strong signs of English influence, in the form of late medieval style houses. All of these styles reflected the European origins of the settlers, who tried to recreate the homes of the mother country using local materials. In the Spanish colonies of Texas, Arizona, New Mexico and California, Spanish Baroque was predictably the architectural style, blended with local Indian crafts.

LIFESTYLE

When we look at surviving Baroque interiors today, they can appear rather sombre and heavy; but when they were complete with furniture (which was often silvered or incorporated tortoiseshell), glowing with candlelight and filled with richly dressed and bejewelled guests, they must have been magnificent. There was a sumptuous look to Baroque decoration, with ornate plasterwork, unpainted oak panelling with inset portraits and beautiful woodcarving enriched with gold leaf on staircases, overdoors and balustrades. The work of the woodcarver and sculptor Grinling Gibbons was particularly admired. Dutch by birth, he later settled in England where most of his work was carried out. Tapestries and leather hangings were other means of embellishment. Towards the end of the century, walls and ceilings decorated with allegorical paintings became fashionable. An extraordinary vogue for Chinese porcelain had also developed by then. The use of an abundance of fabric gave rooms a welcoming feel. Mirrors, particularly huge pier-glasses, were used a great deal.

Baroque houses were laid out in much the same pattern all over Europe. The greater the intimacy of a visitor with the occupants, the deeper into the house he could penetrate. As one progressed through the sequence of rooms, the size of the rooms diminished but the decoration and furniture became richer. The ultimate was the closet or "cabinet" room beyond the bedchamber; this relatively small room would contain the finest velvets, porcelain and paintings.

Individually, the rooms were laid out so as to impress the visitor, though comfort was increasingly a priority. The arrangement of furniture was formal, with a complete absence of furniture in the centre of the room. Chairs were placed in regimented rows with their backs to the wall and were only pulled out when actually being used. One of Louis XIV's mistresses apparently incurred his wrath when she left a chair she had been using in the middle of the room. Sometimes chairs were lined up in close array to make a striking band of colour. Beds were placed with the head against the wall so they projected into the room. Important beds were frequently set on a raised dais, and, in France, often had a balustrade to prevent people of lesser rank from getting too close. French ladies even received guests from their beds; the guests would sit round on stools.

The cost of materials was high. Most fabrics were still imported and were all handmade, a very time-consuming process. Because of their inevitable expense all finished articles were very carefully protected. Chairs had removable slip-covers, while beds had protective "case" curtains and wall hangings. Since many of the grand houses were only occupied on a seasonal basis, the interiors were covered in dust sheets for much of the year and only brought to life when the family was in residence. It was usual to have rich hangings such as tapestry or velvet for the winter and lighter silks for summer.

Architects had little say over the interiors of this period, and the upholsterer was all-important. The upholsterer brought a unified look to rooms long before architects designed all the interior elements as a total scheme. They were in effect interior decorators commissioning a large number of different trades. It was fashionable for the interiors and exteriors of buildings to be coordinated. (In France this even extended to garden design.)

Rare late 17th century wall hangings at Knole in Kent. The window is framed with a shaped pelmet, which was fashionable in France at this time, but on the whole English window treatments were still very basic, like the simple muslin curtains used here.

Opposite: Sumptuous wall hangings were a feature of Baroque homes. Often tapestries were cut to fit the dimensions and architectural features of the room in which they were hung. This is Southside House in south London, built in 1665.

In the early 1600s there was little upholstery on chairs, so an upholsterer would have mainly been involved with arranging hangings to fit a particular room. These hangings could be of tapestry or fabric stretched on the walls. Wall hangings, particularly in France, were increasingly spectacular and sophisticated, with tapestry, velvet and silk damask all very prevalent. At Versailles the upholsterer Delobel designed what was really a mural of fabric of The Triumph of Venus. Wall treatments and portières were sometimes linked by a continuous pelmet, and panels of fabric could have miniature pelmets at the top to finish them off.

Furniture and Upholstery

Cushions were at this time a great luxury and a sign of high status and of a life of leisure. They were often fringed and had ornate tassels at the corners. Cane or rush seats were softened with cushions, which were sometimes attached to the chairs with ribbons. The Moorish tradition of using cushions on the floor was adopted in France as well as in England.

As the century progressed, farthingale chairs, with padded seats and backs, appeared. Often used for dining, these were the first chairs with fixed upholstery. They usually had nail patterning and were covered in leather or "Turkeywork". (Turkeywork was a form of imitation Oriental carpet, made of hand-knotted wool on a canvas backing with patterns copied from Turkish carpets. The colours were very strong and there was nothing subtle about the resulting effect.) Its use was mainly confined to seat upholstery and backstools (stools with added backs).

Early in the century the fashion for voluminous skirts, known as farthingales, led to the appearance of the so-called farthingale chair, which was armless and had a seat wide enough to accommodate this cumbersome apparel.

Oriental carpets, imported by the East India Company, were still used more often on tables than on floors in the 17th century. This table carpet of the period shows a rich combination of gold, blues, reds and browns.

By the 1670s comfortable easy chairs had been developed. They took the form of well-padded armchairs with cheeks and wings and even adjustable backs, and were generally used in more intimate rooms such as bedchambers and closets. X-frame chairs were mainly used as chairs of state and, like most chairs in the grander houses, would have been covered in silk damask or silk velvet. By the end of the century, horsehair was being used to fill mattresses and to pad furniture. It was held in place by buttoning or quilting.

Furniture was increasingly designed for comfort and practicality. Walnut became the fashionable wood, often inlaid with marquetry. Silvered furniture and Oriental lacquer were highly popular.

Colours

Colours favoured in the 17th century were generally rich and sombre, and it was fashionable to use contrasting colours for effect. Combinations included gold with bright blue, green and violet; deep pink with white, red and green; olive green with yellow; and crimson with ivory or white (possibly one of the most popular mixes).

Fashions in colour and texture were as important in costume as in interior decoration. Materials and trimmings became increasingly rich, reflecting the fact that homes and clothing were both widely regarded as status symbols.

Chairs became more comfortable during the 17th century as fixed upholstery developed. This chair with seat cushion and padded back and arms covered in an embroidered fabric is from the second quarter of the 17th century.

American Interiors

A typical New England interior of the late 17th century, with a floor of wide planks and a low ceiling. The huge fireplace would have been used for cooking as well as heating the house. As in Europe, valued Persian carpets were used more on tables than on floors.

In the American colonies during what has been termed the Pilgrim Century (1607–1685), interiors, like the architecture, were influenced by the original nationality of the settlers. The Baroque style did not feature in North America at this time, as fashions had not yet started crossing the Atlantic.

The typical frame house of New England generally consisted of a room on each side of a large central chimney. Next to the chimney were narrow winding stairs leading up to the attic. The enormous open fireplace was used for cooking as well as heating. Ceilings were low, the oak beams were exposed and the walls were unpainted or whitewashed lath and plaster. The wood-framed casement windows were small, with leaded panes. Floors consisted of wide planks, and animal skins provided floor coverings.

The cottages of the Huguenot and Flemish settlers in the Hudson River region were exceptionally long and low, with steeply pitched roofs and extended leaves. The tall, narrow New York Dutch town houses, built of brick and with stepped-gable ends, had higher ceilings and larger windows, as well as horizontally divided doors, built-in beds, and Delft tiles.

It is thought that the houses in Virginia and the South were small versions of the English Jacobean manor, though almost none have survived. They may have had panelled walls and ornamental plasterwork. In these Southern houses the chimneys would have been at the ends of the house.

The wealthier colonial families had imported English furniture, particularly those in the South, which had the closest links with England, but more modest homes used locally made pieces. This furniture was essentially Jacobean in style, long after the end of the Jacobean era in England. Oak was the wood most commonly used at first, but by the second half of the century walnut, maple and pine were also used.

Furniture was decorated with simple carved and turned ornament and some earth colours. Pieces included bedsteads; court cupboards; chests; furniture appropriate to the limited space, such as trestle, fold-up and frame tables with detachable tops, and a hinged-back chair which could be converted into a table; stools and benches; wooden- or rush-seated chairs with cushions. The upholstered backstool known as a Cromwellian chair appeared towards the end of the century.

This fine oak bed, from the early to mid 17th century, has a carved and panelled headboard and tester, with crewel work bed curtains and bed cover. This type of furniture was often used by the American settlers to furnish their homes in the New World, and the Jacobean style persisted there long after the end of the era in England.

Detail of the Baroque canopy and hangings of the bed in the State Bedroom at Clandon Park, Surrey. Trimmings for drapery had become highly complex by the late 17th century, and this valance is richly decorated.

CURTAINS AND DRAPERY

Opposite: William III's recently restored tall and narrow bed at Hampton Court, London. The King bought the bed secondhand from a nearby house! The main hangings are in red velvet and the case curtains in taffeta lustring on a double gilded rod. The remaining original headboard looks like silver but is in fact dirty gold lace. The ostrich plumes are copied from the originals.

This was a century of major development for curtains and draperies. In France the Louis XIII and XIV styles produced highly decorative curtains for beds and windows. In England the window curtain was still a fairly rare sight until the second half of the century, but bed drapery was now of considerable magnificence. The arrival of the sash window, which gave new light and symmetry to both exterior and interior, brought the decoration of the window more into focus. Although early forms of curtaining were quite basic – often just a single curtain in thin fabric, crudely hung – by the end of the century, paired curtains were in use and it had become fashionable to decorate beds, curtains and chairs *en suite* in dark, rich colours. A new innovation in window treatments at this time was the pull-up curtain. This sort of luxury was however, confined to the wealthiest homes.

Beds and Bed Hangings

A simple but elegant four-poster bed of the period, with white and red hangings and a plain red damask bed cover.

Beds remained of great importance and a symbol of the wealth and status of their owner. There were various types of beds, including trundle or truckle beds set on wheels so that they could be stowed away and travelling "field" beds for military men. The beds known as French beds had a simple wooden framework which would be completely covered by the hangings; there was no cornice around the top of the frame, and the curtains hung straight down from the rails, being held in place with nails. There were domed testers; *lits à la duchesse*, which were really half-testers, with a "flying" canopy suspended over the head of the bed by cords attached to the ceiling; and special beds to fit under a sloping roof in the servants' rooms.

Another type of bed was the daybed. Fashionable in France and England, daybeds could be used with canopies as couches for receiving guests, but their chief attraction was as a place to relax away from the rigid formality of court life. In any case, they were a luxury and a symbol of wealth and power, and the hangings were often enriched with gold lace, pearls and gold embroidery as well as plumes and gilded and sculptured cornices.

At the beginning of the century beds were usually placed in the corner of the room, but as the century progressed they gradually moved to a central point on the wall. As a general rule, servants' beds were hidden away in odd corners. They often slept on pallets made of straw covered in ticking or canvas, which were stowed away in large chests when not in use. It was not unusual for a personal servant to sleep at the door of a master or mistress.

Most beds were made of wood, though in hospitals iron bedsteads were used, and in Denmark attractive basketwork beds were introduced for the home. Beds were growing taller, and the French influence was evident in the sumptuous fabrics and trimmings used for the hangings. A bed made for Queen Anne at Hampton Court Palace shortly before her death had a three-metre (ten-foot) high frame and magnificent crimson, gold and ivory cut-silk hangings believed to have been woven at London's Spitalfields, the British silk-weaving centre.

The number of actual curtains used for bed hangings was either two, four or six. It was customary to hang fabric below the top rail of a tester bed and this became known as a "valance" – a term also used to indicate the back part of a helmet worn in tropical countries for protection against the sun. Nowadays the term is used not only for a part of the bed hangings but also to describe any softly pleated pelmet. The inner

Far left: An example of a 17th century *lit à la duchesse,* or angel bed. The "flying" canopy is suspended by cords attached to the ceiling and so does not require endposts.

Left: A Louis XIV domed tester bed, the canopy covered in fabric and topped with carving and plumed ostrich feathers.

and outer valances of 17th century beds were richly decorated and the hangings were often lined in a contrasting colour. The hangings were sometimes magnificently decorated with crewelwork or other forms of embroidery. Counterpanes too could be richly embroidered or occasionally delicately worked with appliquéd patterns. Turned knobs were often fitted above the tester and could be carved, gilded or covered with fabric and trimmed. Beds were also decorated with white or coloured sprigs, aigrettes of feathers or ostrich plumes, or enchanting little artificial bouquets of flowers in silk or metal. It was customary, at this time, to decorate beds, curtains and chairs *en suite* (all in the same fabric).

As an alternative to curtains, fabric was sometimes simply draped around the bedposts. This would have been less of a fire hazard from candles but would not have kept the occupant as warm as hanging curtains. Sheets were mainly white in England but were sometimes striped or checked on the Continent. An interesting practical feature of the period was "bed staves", clever wooden pins to stop the bedclothes from slipping off. A similar device using combs was found in Sweden.

Windows

Casement windows, in use since medieval times, have never really been out of fashion. But the 1600s saw great changes in the window in England. It gradually became narrower and the central mullion disappeared. As the century progressed these refinements went still further until by 1640 the sliding-sash window had evolved. Initially it had only a single sliding sash held open by catches at the side, but soon a double-hung sash with a counterbalance system of weights with pulleys was developed – a system which has hardly changed to the present day. Glazing bars were very broad, and were left unpainted. This type of window was a major innovation; its symmetry, combined with the increased light it provided, was a major influence on the development of interior furnishing and curtaining in particular.

Glass was quite readily available now, and by the end of the century most windows were glazed. It was sometimes fashionable to have scenes and figures painted on the inside of the glass or to have inserted stained-glass panels featuring coats of arms. This was particularly popular in Holland, Flanders and England.

Curtains

In 17th century England, curtains at the windows were still uncommon and really only found in rooms of importance in the grandest homes. Privacy was not a problem in country houses, though shutters were often used on the first and second floors of town houses for this reason. The cold, however, was a universal problem, and sometimes mats or special window cloths were fitted into the window recess to keep out draughts; these were hooked into place at night.

A shaped quilted pelmet with braid and fringe in the Louis XIV style makes a pleasing frame to this window.

Paired curtains remained rare until the latter part of the century. The idea of dividing the single curtain down the middle so that the two halves could be drawn to opposite sides of the window came when architectural styles demanded a symmetrical effect. Some of the earliest paired curtains were recorded at Ham House in 1654, and by the 1670s all the principal rooms at Ham had been fitted with them.

Even in the wealthiest houses curtains were not as lavish as the bed hangings. They were often made of sarsnet, a thin type of silk taffeta. In simpler homes, if curtains were used at all, they would probably have been of a worsted wool in blue or another dark colour. Dark colours were rather nicely referred to as "sad".

One of the major influences on window treatments at this time was Daniel Marot. He had worked in the French royal drawing office but during the time of religious persecution he went into exile in Holland, where he worked for the Dutch royal family. Brought over to England by William and Mary of Orange, he worked at Hampton Court and other royal palaces at the end of the century. Marot liked to give a unity of design to a room, and his engravings were very influential. He favoured portières *en suite* with wall hangings, a combination which was not only decorative but also functional as it excluded draughts. Portières were much used in France at this time and were often beautifully decorated with appliqué work.

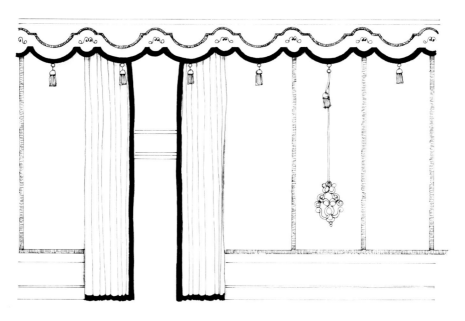

Wall hangings and portière curtains unified by a continuous shaped pelmet in the style of Daniel Marot, a designer who was very influential around the end of the century. The seams of the wall hangings are disguised with braid.

It was not unusual for portières to be combined with flat, shaped, stiffened pelmets. The French called these "lambrequins", a direct translation of which is "scallop", so it is reasonable to suppose that the name was based on the shape. There was also, however, a special harness for horses which was highly decorative and usually had scalloped edges and which was also called "lambrequin", so it may have inspired identical models in interior decoration. (The English term "pelmet" is almost interchangeable with lambrequin, though nowadays a lambrequin usually drops down on either side of a window. The guiding feature in the shaping of a lambrequin is the pattern of the fabric. Pelmets or lambrequins are attached to a pelmet board and fixed with either tacks, hooks-and-eyes or occasionally Velcro.)

One of the major innovations of the century was pull-up curtains, in other words, curtains that pulled up by means of cords to hang in festoons or swags. Daniel Marot excelled at them. Restrained and elegant, they possibly developed from the tie-up curtains used on beds.

White silk damask pull-up curtains in the style of Daniel Marot, at London's recently restored Hampton Court, where Marot worked for William and Mary at the end of the 17th century. The damask has been specially woven and the curtains constructed in accordance with inventories to ensure they are as similar as possible to Marot's originals.

Their advantage was that they looked good from both the interior and the exterior of a building if not pulled up too tightly against the top of the window. Usually made of silk, they were unlined and, when pulled down, hung flat across the window with no gathering. They were designed to pull up against the under surface of the top of the window. The curtain was nailed to the front edge of the pulley board, with a ruffled heading rising a few centimetres (an inch or two) above the board. The architecture of the period allowed them to rest between the top of the window architrave and the ceiling cornice without spoiling the line of the window or blocking out too much light, unlike so many of the 20th-century versions.

To complement hanging curtains, Daniel Marot designed elaborately gathered and festooned pelmets like these.

As the century progressed, the pulley board was topped with a shaped window cornice sometimes covered with curtain fabric. Hanging curtains were still in use, and pelmets and valances were introduced. Stiffened, shaped and ornamented pelmets, often trimmed with tassels for definition, were highly fashionable. Daniel Marot designed complex pelmets with gathered pleats falling into festoons and tails. One of the earliest forms of pelmet for decorative purposes consisted of a short, fringed, skirt-like curtain which occupied a place at the top of a curtained or fabric-covered wall, over a window, at the edge of a canopy or attached to the edge of a chair or bench.

From the middle of the century, white silk blinds were used in grander houses to protect the interior fittings and furniture from the sun. Holland matting and unlined Indian calico were also used. When the calico was painted it looked very pretty with sunlight shining through it. At Versailles white damask blinds shot with gold thread were employed, and by the end of the century in France external slatted blinds were in use.

Sashes were another form of sunblind. The fabric was stretched on a wooden frame and soaked in oil or turpentine for a translucent look. They were tinted green or some other dark colour and were often painted with scenes or designs. Occasionally they were hinged. In 1640 the double windows of the Chambre du Roi at Fontainebleau were fitted with decorative sashes made of paper. In Stockholm sashes were fitted outside windows, but they were very rarely used in England except for special festive occasions, when candles would be lit behind them.

In the 17th century there was a wealth of wonderful figured silks, such as this taffeta in a ribbon and flower design.

Fabrics

There was a surprisingly large range of fabrics available at this time. In England they were mostly imported from Italy, France and Flanders. The simpler fabrics included tickings, used for mattresses, bolsters and pillows; linen for backings, linings and bed and table linen; and sackcloth for chair padding. Cotton was much used for upholstery. Colourful Indian hand-painted and printed cottons which were known in France as *indiennes* (see page 21) and which were an early form of chintz, were initially used as table carpets and stool covers, and later as curtains, bed and wall hangings and bed covers.

Of the more expensive fabrics, damasks of silk, linen or wool were still much favoured for the way the pattern of two contrasting weaves caught the light. Silks of all types abounded. There were plain silks, ribbed silks, watered silks, silks dyed with a clouded effect, silks with gold thread woven through them, silk taffetas and sarsnet, a thin type of silk taffeta much used for early window curtains. All silks could be brocaded. The French were partial to heavy taffetas and moirés. The

This upholstered window seat banked with cushions has a distinctly 17th century feel. Cushions, often fringed, were a status symbol and luxury, and the elaborate trimmings and rich colours are also characteristic of the period. Paired curtains were well established by the end of the century, and tie-backs were usually made of cord.

silk industry in England was mainly developed by French and Dutch weavers and further advanced by the Huguenot refugees who settled in Norwich, Canterbury and the Spitalfields area of London. Spitalfields became the main British centre for silk damasks and brocades.

At the top of the range were exquisite, bold-patterned Genoa velvets from either Genoa or Lyons and the *gaufrage* velvets with the pattern stamped on with heated metal. *Gaufrage* velvets are currently enjoying a popular revival. Brocatelle, a fabric with poor draping qualities, and tapestry were mainly used for wall hangings. Hangings could also be printed, painted or flocked.

Leather, most of which was imported from Turkey and Morocco, was widely used in interiors at this time for wall hangings and chair coverings. It was frequently embossed with a wooden mould or punched with small sub-patterns to reflect light. The main part of a pattern could be painted in one or more colours, then the unpainted sections would be glazed with yellow varnish, imparting a gilded effect.

In the mid 17th century the first Provençal prints, copies of the popular imported *indiennes*, were produced by printing with carved wooden blocks on cotton, and an industry of mixed fortunes was launched. Their early success was thought to be threatening the weavers' trade and so from 1692 their importation into France from Marseilles and Avignon (which were under papal rule and outside French jurisdiction) was prohibited. As a result the industry temporarily declined until the ban was lifted in the mid 18th century.

Heraldic patterns were used in textiles in the 17th century, but more for their decorative effect than for any symbolic meaning. Needlepoint played an important part in the soft furnishings of a house, and work carried out in petit-point (small stitches), which was particularly hard-wearing, was suitable for chair covers when used with a canvas backing. During England's Restoration period, stumpwork, with its raised, padded patterns and multitude of stitches, was used for such purposes as panel pictures or the decoration of mirrors.

American textiles at this time were predominantly homespun. Linsey-wolsey, a strong, warm fabric, was woven from wool, the main fibre of North America, and linen. By the end of the century, homespun fabrics were being supplemented in very affluent homes by imported woven textiles, such as richly coloured damasks and velvets, which were used for curtains, bed hangings, table covers and seat pads.

Trimmings

There was little trace of decorative trimmings in the 15th and 16th centuries, but by the time of Louis XIV *passementerie* appeared in all the new decorations in the French royal residences.

In general, 17th century trimmings, which were made mainly in wool, silk and linen, had clean lines and became increasingly delicate and complex as the century progressed. Lively, sometimes even frothy, the trimmings exhibited a variety of effects and clever combinations subtly applied. There were velour braids decorated with stylized flowers, lozenges and other geometric patterns, often with the addition of appliqué work or a lace trim. Fringes had braided tops, sometimes with superimposed motifs, and could be enriched with gold or silver tassels which were quite simple, usually with a pear-shaped top. Campaign fringe had bell-like tufts which gave a rich look. Most tie-backs were in the form of rope cord with tassels for definition.

Many of the less standardized trimmings showed great originality and ingenuity. These were particularly devised to finish off upholstery, disguise seams on wall hangings or enhance bed and window hangings. Tapestries were often fringed and enriched with intricate and unusual edgings, such as a border trimmed with puffs of pink silk, or openwork lace adorned with metal wires, creamy strips of parchment and tufts of coloured silk to give a three-dimensional effect. Seams were hidden and large areas of wall divided into panels by the use of metal lace or silver and gold thread applied in bands. Rosettes and ribbons, cords and tassels were used to give definition.

3

THE EARLY TO MID 18TH CENTURY

The Palladian Revival and Rococo

There were two major styles in the early to mid 18th century: the Rococo, which began in Paris and was dominant in Europe, and the Palladian revival, which was primarily English. The Rococo was never fully accepted in England, but many interiors were influenced by it, particularly through plasterwork, smaller decorative pieces such as mirrors and porcelain, and furniture. In addition, the Rococo offshoots – the "Chinese taste" and the "Gothick taste" – were all the rage in England.

In many ways, the two styles could not have been more opposite. The Rococo was frivolous, exuberant, delicate, curvaceous and asymmetrical; the Palladian revival was rigid, restrained, rather heavy and symmetrical. Yet each was elegant in its own way.

INFLUENCES

At the end of Louis XIV's reign in France there was a new feeling of informality and a desire to escape from the rigidity of court life. The Régence (1715–23) – the period when Philip, Duke of Orleans, was Regent to the infant Louis XV – was a time of transition, from Classical arts to a freedom of expression. This first phase of the Rococo developed with the encouragement of the Regent, who was very interested in art and architecture. Although it was primarily a domestic style, there were, nevertheless, some splendid examples of ecclesiastical interiors. The Rococo appealed to European aristocracy as a whole, and foreign rulers and royalty consulted French architects for advice on the construction and decoration of important buildings and palaces.

The columns, pilasters, heavy panelling and overmantels of the Baroque were replaced by rooms with elaborate asymmetrical

Chinoiserie, or the "Chinese Taste", was probably more popular in England than Rococo itself. The State Bedroom at Nostell Priory, Yorkshire, shown here, was decorated by Chippendale in this style. The hand-painted Chinese wallpaper, lacquer furniture and mirror were all supplied by him. The bed and window draperies were added later but are completely in keeping.

47

plasterwork and delicate cornicing contrasting with plain ceilings and paintings above door panels. Mirrors were used lavishly and placed in original and innovative ways. Stucco and tiles were applied instead of wood panelling, and an Italian influence was clearly visible in the use of coloured marble or imitation marble for floors and chimneypieces.

The Rococo (or Louis Quinze style, as it is sometimes called, because its full-blown phase developed during the reign of Louis XV) burgeoned in Paris for the aristocracy. It did not really reach the court of Versailles until the 1730s, however, when the *petits apartements du roi* were executed by the young architect Jacques-Ange Gabriel and the master carver Jacques Verberckt. The Rococo was at its height in France in the 1740s and was much copied in Italy, Spain, Hungary, Austria, Poland and Russia.

It was Germany, however, which took the style to its heart; nowhere in Europe was the Rococo interpreted with such brilliance as in Germany. Two German princes, exiled to Paris after they had colluded with Louis XV over the War of Spanish Succession, took the new ideas back to Germany with them, and there were also many Paris-trained German craftsmen. Yet despite the strong French influence, there were a number of notable differences between the two styles. In general, German Rococo was grand and stately, while French Rococo was more lighthearted, informal and frivolous. A notable feature of the German style was incredibly delicate plasterwork in rooms of all shapes and sizes. French plasterwork, on the other hand, was confined mainly to rectangular rooms. German plasterwork was often so rampant that it obscured the structural lines of the room, rather than defining them in the French manner.

The Baroque style had fallen out of favour in England too, and at the beginning of the 18th century, the brief reign of Queen Anne marked the advent of a new simplicity and elegance, which continued into the Georgian period. There was a return to the Classical ideas of the Venetian architect Andrea Palladio, which Inigo Jones had introduced to England in the previous century. The architect Lord Burlington had brought back engravings of Palladio's original designs on a visit to Italy early in the century, but the original Italian style of Palladian interior decoration did not suit the English taste or climate. A highly successful English compromise was reached with the use of restrained Baroque decoration within Palladian disciplines. William Kent – the architect, interior decorator, furniture designer and landscape gardener who, with his patron Lord Burlington, was the main influence in the Palladian revival – designed appropriate furniture (his chairs have been described as looking like thrones), and the resulting interiors in houses such as Holkham Hall and Houghton Hall in Norfolk and Chiswick House were splendid.

Lord Burlington and his circle of "men of taste" had revolted against the work of Wren and Vanbrugh (see page 26). They asserted that the

William Kent was one of the most influential figures in England during the early 18th century, designing sumptuous interiors and reassuringly solid furniture for Palladian revival houses. His famous bed at Houghton Hall, Norfolk, features an enormous shell (one of his favourite motifs) at the head, along with an equally impressive cornice and fine green velvet curtains.

Palladian revival was a more "natural" style than Baroque because it satisfied the demands of reason. Furthermore, they maintained that the appropriate setting for a neo-Palladian villa should not therefore be the formal, geometric, Versailles type of garden then fashionable, but a deliberately irregular, picturesque English landscape. William Kent designed the "ha-ha", a sunken barrier, so that the vista would not be interrupted by a fence. At the same time, the landscape gardener Lancelot "Capability" Brown changed the face of much of the countryside with his natural-looking landscaped parklands for country estates.

Two variations of Rococo did become fashionable in England, however. Chinoiserie – the "Chinese taste" as it was called, which was a style of decoration based on romanticized, pseudo-Oriental motifs – was popular all over Europe. In England it reached its height in the 1740s and '50s. The second variation on Rococo was equally romanticized and inaccurate: Gothick was a style of architecture and furniture loosely based on medieval Gothic architecture. It appeared in the 1730s but was almost entirely confined to England. Strawberry Hill, near London, Horace Walpole's house which he decorated entirely in this style in the 1740s, was the most influential Gothick house of the day, and a perfect example of the style.

In Colonial America during the first half of the century, the economy grew rapidly and a wealthy merchant middle class emerged. Relatively luxurious houses were built along the Atlantic coast, and a traditional popular taste was developing. The main centres of design were in Philadelphia, Newport, Boston, Baltimore, Maryland, New York and Salem. By the middle of the century, town houses tended to be very elaborate, often with light, curving staircases in contrast to their stolid predecessors. Country homes, however, were much simpler.

The Colonial styles tended to mirror the fashions in England, though usually with a time lag. William and Mary interiors were favoured in the early part of the century, and Queen Anne style from around 1720 to 1750. The Palladian revival did not really develop there until after 1750. There were some glimpses of Rococo, particularly chinoiserie, but once again they did not develop before the second half of the century. Outside of the wealthy South, large mansions were rare.

LIFESTYLE

Paris was at this time the centre of European culture, and most countries on the Continent imitated its fashions. Life for the court and high society was intimate, informal, glittering and hedonistic. Women dominated the social life, and great store was set by wit, poise, the art of conversation, and the ability to please. The charming, lighthearted paintings of artists of the period like Watteau, Fragonard and Boucher reflected those attitudes, as did the aristocratic and frivolous Rococo style. The French queen, wife of Louis XV and daughter of the deposed King of Poland, introduced into the court a new dance, which became known as the Polonaise. This was sufficiently energetic to require the ladies to hitch up their dresses, leading to a new style of dress – the Polonaise – in which the skirt could be looped up. This idea of catching things up filtered through to the bed and window treatments of the day.

In England, by contrast, the court had little prestige or influence on the arts. The landed aristocracy, who were mainly Whigs, wanted comfort, convenience, and a little splendour in their homes. Women were not as dominant in English society as they were in France. Consequently, Rococo decoration slipped in as a decorative novelty rather than emerging as a reflection of the fundamental attitudes of the time. The main preoccupation was showing the "correct taste", and the elegant, restrained Palladian revival accurately echoed this.

As a result of the ever-increasing wealth of the upper classes at this time, and their desire for culture and a classical education, the Grand Tour became an important part of life in the 1700s. The wealthy travelled extensively, returning with inspiring ideas and wonderful treasures. Their passion for collecting paintings of Italian masters often reduced some English rooms to mere galleries.

French Rococo

The full Rococo style of interior decoration that was so fashionable in France and the rest of the Continent towards the middle of the century was one of charm and fantasy, in keeping with the new mood of informality and desire for comfort. Light played a vital part in these schemes, and mirrors were used to reflect daylight and candlelight, often being placed above marble mantelpieces and as pier glasses above console tables. Plasterwork was free-flowing and often asymmetrical, and friezes were of garlands, flowers and, especially, shells. (The *rocaille* – shell- or rock-work – was the most characteristic Rococo motif.)

Windows and doors were round or open-headed with depressed arches, and wall panels were often painted with decorative motifs. Floors were mainly of patterned marble or wooden block, though earthen floors were still common in country homes. Popular motifs, many of which were inspired by nature, included humorous monkeys and dragons. An innovation that has remained popular to the present day was the idea of a symmetrical display on the mantelpiece, usually with a large clock in the centre, flanked by a matching pair of porcelain vases. Wall-hung brackets used for the display of vases were also a feature of the period.

A phrase used to describe these styles was *"le genre pittoresque"*, which was how the painter Charles Coypel spoke of the engravings of Meissonnier in his book *Livre d'Ornaments*. Meissonnier, who trained

Informality, frivolity and charm characterized the Rococo style, which originated in Paris. Hangings were light and elegant, as in this French Rococo bed.

A day bed set in an alcove that has been softly swagged and hung with curtains caught back at the sides. In Rococo France, beds and sofas were often given a similar treatment, being set in alcoves decorated with side curtains held back by cords.

as a goldsmith, was a leading designer of Rococo ornaments and furniture featuring shell- and rock-work combined with forms like foliage, water and carved rocks.

French furniture dealers employed independent designers and craftsmen to fulfil commissions from royalty and the aristocracy and, in this way, exercised considerable influence over taste and style. Surprisingly, in strict contrast to the informality of the Rococo style, furniture of the period still tended to be arranged around the room in a very rigid and symmetrical fashion.

English Rococo

The offshoots of the Rococo style, namely chinoiserie and Gothick, appealed to the English more than the Rococo itself. These specialized styles were seen in furniture and decoration – for example, in the popular hand-painted Chinese wallpaper and lacquered furniture – but hardly ever as an integral part of a scheme.

Ceilings were sometimes painted, and decorative plasterwork, where used, was generally in white and gold. Stucco, with its finer finish, had been practically unknown in England before the 18th century and now became very fashionable. It was ideally suited to the sinuous scrollwork of a Rococo ceiling, which was one Rococo feature that did make its way across the English Channel.

Some English furniture was designed in the Rococo style, and pieces could be seen in the influential pattern-book *The Gentleman and Cabinet-Maker's Director*, first published in 1754 by Thomas Chippendale. Chippendale's name is universally associated with English Rococo furniture (see page 54).

The Palladian Revival

In England, the first half of the 18th century was a time of great development in interior decoration, architecture and landscape gardening. In the early part of the century English interiors were simple and elegant; the Queen Anne period (1702–1714) at the beginning of the Palladian revival is synonymous with good taste and understatement. Windows were treated as part of the whole decorative scheme, and in some houses there was a move towards smaller rooms with lower ceilings and a more intimate feel. Privacy was becoming a higher priority.

In the 1720s and '30s country houses were built in England in the formal Palladian style, with the main rooms, which had slightly higher ceilings, not on the ground floor but on the first floor. This main floor, or *piano nobile* ("noble floor"), was most often approached by a grand, impressive staircase. There was usually a large apartment on this floor with a state bedroom and a chamber of state, preceded by two or three rooms such as a drawing-room and a presence chamber and followed by a dressing-room and closet. Other essential family rooms such as a library and a music room could be sited on this or other floors. The rusticated basement storey, at ground-floor level, was known as the "rustic" and contained the kitchen, cellars, service rooms and, often, informal living rooms.

The Palladian-revival style of interior decoration was lavish yet tasteful. One of the great advantages of this style was the way it lent itself to simplification and scaling down if necessary for the smaller interior. As with the buildings themselves, balance and symmetry were keynotes in the interiors. The interior architectural details – Classical pediments, imposing ceilings and cornices – were important features.

To contrast with textile hangings, the woodwork of door and window frames and cornicing would be pale-coloured with gold detailing. At the beginning of the century, walls were still panelled, though pine had largely taken over from the more expensive oak. Whereas oak had simply been waxed, the pine was painted with an eggshell-finish paint, or it was grained or marbled to simulate high-quality materials. By around 1740, panelling had fallen out of fashion. Walls were then increasingly painted in a matt finish, or hung with wallpaper or dark silk or velvet. The wall hangings were now fixed. Walls were first lined with wood for warmth and then covered with canvas and lining paper and finally the fabric itself. Alternatively, the fabric was stretched over a wooden frame attached directly to the rough-plastered wall.

Whereas previouly wallpaper was used by the middle and lower classes but not the upper classes, who preferred textiles, this suddenly changed early in the 18th century. Flocked wallpapers, which had been manufactured since the late 17th century, became all the rage in England when William Kent used them to replace textile hangings in the King's Great Drawing Room at Kensington Palace. A crimson flocked paper used in the Whitehall Offices of the Privy Council became the favoured paper for the grand rooms of Palladian-revival houses. Flocked papers were also exported to France, where the fashion-conscious eagerly removed their Gobelin tapestries to make way for them.

This description of Eastby by Mrs. Lybbe Powys gives a very good idea of a typical Georgian interior.

Having ascended a grand flight of steps you come under a Doric Portico whose pediment extends 62 feet with pillars 46 feet high; from thence you enter a noble hall adorned by statues and busts, the saloon painted olive, the ornaments, as the cornice of rich gilt; the sofas in this apartment are very fine tapestry. On one side of the saloon is the common dining-room, and drawing-room and on the other the best drawing-room hung with silk and furnished with cut velvet; the state bedchamber hung with crimson velvet furniture, the bed with gold and lin'd with a painted Indian satin; the dressing-room hung with green satin.

The Managareth or Chinese bedroom and dressing-room in the attic storey is excessively droll and pretty, furnish'd exactly as in China, the bed of an uncommon size, seven feet wide by six long.

Furniture and Upholstery

Furniture thought to be suitable for a Palladian-revival house was fairly massive, rigid and restrained, with pediments, cornices, lion masks and paws, swags, etc. William Kent was the most important designer. (Palladio himself is not believed to have designed any furniture.)

Thomas Chippendale was of course the best-known English furniture designer, and the publication of his *Director* in the middle of

Crimson damask pull-up curtains, pelmets, wall coverings and upholstery complement the coved and coffered ceiling in William Kent House, a London town house designed by William Kent in the Palladian style.

A Toylet Table

J. Chippendale invᵗ et delinᵗ.   Publish'd according to Act of Parliament 1760.   Morris sculp.

the century made him a household name. Most of the designs in it were Rococo, and there were also some of the chinoiserie type known as Chinese Chippendale. He also applied Gothick window-tracery, pinnacles and crockets to furniture that was otherwise Classical in design. His finest furniture, however, was produced after 1765 in the Neoclassical Adam style.

By the middle of the century, mahogany had largely replaced walnut as the favoured wood for furniture.

The most successful upholsterers in the early 18th century came from France; many upholsterers employed in the royal palaces in England had French names. While it was relatively simple to pad a chair and secure a cover over it with nails around the edge, distortion caused many difficulties, especially on chair backs. In Italy and Spain a special fish-scale design was developed in order to help combat this problem.

Comfort became a priority, with drop-in seats and seats padded with deep cushions. Wing armchairs were increasingly popular from the reign of Queen Anne onwards, and occasional chairs were tall and elegant, sometimes with cabriole legs.

Silk was the most widely used covering in the grander homes of the time, but linen and printed cottons were also used. Chairs were often supplied with two sets of covers, something light and informal for the summer and often silk damask coverings for the winter months. Although pastel shades were used for these a great deal, stronger colours such as magenta, deep green and royal blue were to be found in fashionable society.

Turkeywork was still in vogue for the covering of back stools, as was the use of leather. The nailing patterns on these could be decorative, often incorporating round-headed nails of two different sizes. All upholstery techniques (except springing and certain stitched edges) had evolved by 1700.

It was at about this time in France that draped dressing tables appeared. In keeping with the Rococo style, they were given full bouffant and frilled skirts and decorated with ribbons and flowers. Sometimes they came complete with their own canopies to complement the existing sumptuous furnishings.

Colours

There was a generous palette of colours in the early to mid 18th century. In France the Rococo style used delicate colours such as pink, white, yellow, azure blue and ivory mixed with cream and gold. Appliqué on clear colours was fashionable.

In England pine panelling was usually painted in brown, grey, olive green or off-white and mouldings were picked out in gilt. Following this, walls were similarly painted in muted tones like white, stone, drab or olive, as well as in brighter colours like "pea green" (actually the

Charmingly draped dressing tables, decorated with flowers and ribbons, like this one designed by Chippendale around the middle of the century, appeared during the Rococo period.

American homes were becoming more sophisticated by the early 18th century but the curtains, furniture and other furnishings were simpler than in Europe. Homes were generally small, so space was used to the full, as with the fold-up bed in this New Hampshire room of the period. The early 18th century hangings are of homespun linen with crewel embroidery.

bright green of uncooked peas), sky blue, straw, yellow and deep green. Chocolate brown – though not usually associated with the early Georgian period – was often used on internal woodwork, particularly doors and skirting boards (baseboards).

Printed fabrics came in reds, browns, purples and black, and silks and velvets in green, blue and gold. Imported calicoes from India were in a range of strong glowing colours – crimson to shell-pink, deep violet to pale lavender, indigo blue, lemon yellow and sage green – and these in turn influenced the schemes of interiors where they were used.

Many American colours were influenced by the British ones. Their paints, however, had more sheen than the eggshell (and, from the 1740s, matt) paints of Georgian England, as the American pigments were mixed with milk. Their colours included yellow ochre, blue-grey, ox-blood red and deep blue-green, often teamed with burnt sienna.

American Interiors

Colonial American homes had now become more sophisticated. Sir Christopher Wren's influence was apparent in the symmetrically designed houses and Classically arranged interiors of the colonies.

Walls were usually panelled, and the panelling was generally painted in strong, deep tones, used either on their own or in combination. Woven carpets were rare, but stretched canvas floor coverings were painted in imitation of them. Furniture was of walnut and included drop-leaf tables and armless chairs with cabriole legs. Woven and embroidered textiles were now being used in more elaborate ways, not only as draperies but also as upholstery.

CURTAINS AND DRAPERY

The European fashion for Rococo affected curtains and bed hangings – which were lighter, less formal, more frivolous – particularly in France. In Britain, where the Palladian revival predominated, curtains played an important role in decoration for the first time. Drapes were more fashionable than simpler arrangements, and pull-ups were now the height of fashion in England, France and the Netherlands, becoming fuller as the century progressed. Paired curtains with shaped pelmets were still a popular alternative. Beds remained sumptuous, with lavish and exciting trimmings – the ultimate status symbol.

Even the fashions had a very Rococo feel throughout Europe. Motifs on dress fabrics echoed those of the furnishings with ribbons, flowers and shells. Fashionable skirts were so wide that the curved balusters of staircases of this period were specially constructed to allow room for them.

Beds and Bed Hangings

The new informality and intimacy led to the introduction of boudoirs and bedrooms into the private apartments. Beds remained a status symbol and the subject of formidable expenditure. In France it became fashionable to place them in alcoves (sofas were often treated in the same way) but this was never really adopted in England, where the four-poster still reigned supreme. The alcoves were usually decorated with lambrequins and side curtains caught back with rope cord or rosettes.

The *lit à la turque* was introduced. Placed parallel to the wall, it had a small canopy or half-tester above supporting drapery which fell over each end of the bed. Another new style of bed, the *lit à la polonaise*, named after Louis XV's queen, who was Polish, was roofed by a dome held in place by rods from the four corners of the bed or, sometimes, from brackets attached to the wall behind. These styles were introduced in France and subsequently adopted in England and elsewhere.

Bed hangings tended to be lighter, simpler and more elegant than the heavy, ornate versions of the 17th century. By mid-century they were presented as a waterfall of fabric caught back in choux. Valances and bedcovers were cut in elegant shapes, often with a raised appliquéd trimming rather than fringing.

Opposite: An enchanting interpretation of a *lit à la polonaise.* The shaped tester is circular and the delicate drapery is caught back high up the bed posts.

Far left: An 18th century *lit à la polonaise.*

Left: In the *lit à la turque*, which also appeared at this time, the drapery fell from a small canopy over the ends of the bed.

A modern interpretation of the 18th century French idea of placing a bed in an alcove, which is in this case formed by elegant tied-back curtains. The bed cover and under-drapery are in matching fabric.

Windows

At the beginning of the 18th century, the four-light transom casement window with rectangular leaded panes was the most widely used window in Britain. But the sash window complete with internal folding shutters soon became highly popular. Although sash windows had originally been set flush with the outside wall surface, the 1709 Building Act required them to be inset by at least 100mm (4 inches) to reduce the fire risk. This radically changed the exterior appearance of a building and, though the Act was enforced only in London, it was responsible for the look we associate with the architecture of the period. These recessed windows were usually fitted with interior shutters. Glazing bars became narrower, and the glass panes were held in place with putty and metal springs. Windows were usually painted

A bed dressed as a sofa for the daytime in a curtained alcove turns this library into a versatile dual-purpose room. The valance on the alcove is made from a patterned fabric to contrast with the plain fabric of the curtains.

In this original curtain treatment, inspired by 18th century styles, the shallow swag provides a softening effect and, along with the curtains, frames the window and the antique rocking horse.

white at this time where previously they had been left unpainted. This was because the soft wood now used instead of oak for their construction required paint cladding for protection from the elements.

The classic 12-pane (or six-over-six, as it's known in America) sash window became the standard in both Britain and the American colonies, although nine and 15 panes were also common. Proportions were defined by Palladian principles: the windows on the *piano nobile* were double squares (the height was twice the width) while those on the bedroom floor above were one-and-a-quarter times as high as they were wide, and the windows in the attic were square.

The Venetian, or Palladian, window, with a central round-arched section flanked by two narrower side sections, became common now. It was most often fitted at *piano nobile* level.

Curtains

In the early part of the century, shutters were still widely used. Pull-ups remained popular, having become a little fuller, with more ornate trimmings. They were particularly suitable for the tall, narrow sash windows, as they allowed the architecture to be seen. The workings were usually hidden by a pelmet cornice and valance. They were generally made of light fabrics such as taffeta or cotton chintz, but sometimes heavy fabrics such as velvet were used.

Paired curtains were also still in use, often topped with elegantly shaped and stiffened pelmets with appliqué or embroidery work. The French particularly favoured appliqué as a form of decoration at this time. There was now more of a feeling of movement in the way the fabrics were used and in the fabric designs themselves, which often included Rococo motifs such as garlands of flowers, knots of ribbons and fronds of leaves. By the middle of the century pelmets had softened considerably, with shallow swagging and small tails and bells. Portières had deeper pelmets and lighter curtains which were caught back about three-quarters of the way up in the "Italian" style. Light silk festoons (called store marquise) were used in conjunction with draped pelmets. The French handled these styles with a lightness of touch that was sometimes lacking in the heavier British approach.

Roller blinds appeared at this time. Some were recorded in Sweden as early as 1713 while in London they were first used in 1726.

The Venetian windows often installed in Palladian mansions posed a difficult problem for the upholsterer. Thomas Chippendale used a curved pelmet board on the main section on which to fix swags and then straight boards on the two side sections for the tails.

Fabrics

There was an even larger and more sophisticated range of fabrics to choose from in the 18th century. The silk industry was thriving in Europe, with Lyons dominating. Originally their designs had been based on the symmetrical patterns of Italian silks but now scallop and lace effects were incorporated, as were fragile floral patterns and designs incorporating turtle-doves and musical instruments. Silk and its derivatives remained the most used fabric in grand interiors, with linen for beds and tables, backings, linings and inner covers.

Bed hangings too were usually of silk or the rich Genoese silk velvet with its bold patterns rendered in one or more colours in silk pile against a plain or satin ground. This was also now a popular choice for wall coverings. However, it was still terribly expensive due to the amount of work involved in its production. For windows, silk damasks and brocades were used, sometimes with a shimmer of gold thread – the beauty and skill of French embroidery were renowned throughout Europe. Brocatelle was still used for hangings. Satin, taffeta (in particular a type of taffeta called lustring), ribbed silk sometimes with

A mid 18th century treatment for a doorway, showing the new deeper pelmet of the period and the lighter paired curtains caught back in the Italian style.

a glittering finish achieved by being smeared with beer over a brazier, clouded silks with dyed patterns on the warp, and, as the century advanced, chintz, were all used for curtains. In more modest homes woollen stuffs, moreens, harateens and serge would have been used for beds and window draperies. Good plain materials in sober colours included plain leather, silk mohair and plush and velvet for chair coverings.

In earlier centuries, pattern, if not woven into the fabric, had been crudely painted onto the surface, which would not, of course stand up to washing. It was in India that the technique of fixing dyes with mordants (metal salts) to make them colourfast was first perfected. These dyes made it possible to brighten up poor-quality cloth such as calico by hand-painting and printing colourful designs onto it. The resulting fabrics were the *indiennes*, or *chints* (from the Hindu word meaning "speckled") first imported into Marseilles in the late 16th century (see page 21). The importation into Europe of the fabrics continued through the 17th century via the Dutch, English and French East India Companies. As the highly successful trade increased, colours and patterns were adapted to suit European tastes, and patterns were even sent out to India to be copied. These Indian calicoes were the very first chintzes.

Delicate reproduction trimmings in silver. Trimmings of the early 18th century were delicate and charming, and silver satisfied the fashion for glitter. As drapery became fashionable, more weight was required to balance the treatments, and so trimmings became increasingly substantial and dramatic.

By the end of the 17th century, European printworks had been set up to blockprint imitations of these fabrics. The finest chintz was produced at Jouy-en-Josas, outside Versailles, by the Oberkampf factory (which became more famous for its *toiles de Jouy* – see page 96). The technique was also patented in England in 1676 but production was suspended until the 1730s because the weavers felt their trade was threatened. In fact, in both France and England "anti-cloth laws" aimed at protecting the woollen and silk industries held the textile-printing industry back for much of the 18th century. By the 1770s, however, production was in full swing.

America imported chintzes from England until the late 18th century, when it began printing its own. Production was centred around Philadelphia, where English emigrants had set up printworks.

Trimmings

Following the flight of many Huguenots from France in the late 1600s to escape religious persecution, many skilled craftsmen settled in England, Ireland, Germany, Switzerland and the Netherlands, among them upholsterers and exponents of *passementerie*. As a result a wide range of sophisticated trimmings was to be found in these countries in the 18th century. New ideas included the application of broad and narrow bands of gold-coloured lace to a hanging in a rich, contrasting colour, and the use of raised detailing such as gold galloon, frogging or artificial flowers as a trim on pelmets and valances, rather than the heavy fringing of the previous century. Tie-backs, often embroidered or appliquéd and finished with bows and ribbons or tassels, became a feature in their own right.

4

THE LATE 18TH CENTURY

Neoclassicism

The main international style of the second half of the 18th century was Neoclassicism. In most parts of Europe it developed from the 1750s onwards as a reaction to the Rococo style, and was well established by the 1770s. It reached America in the late 1780s. Rational and coolly elegant, it was characterized by a taste for simple geometric forms, flat, linear decoration, and Greek and Roman ornament.

The term Neoclassicism covers a number of different styles, the common factor being their inspiration from the ancient Classical styles of Greece and Rome. The principal sources of this inspiration were the public buildings of Rome and, in particular, the excavations in 1738 and 1748 at Pompeii and Herculaneum. The Renaissance, especially Raphael's painted grotesques at the Vatican, provided another source of inspiration.

For the English, who had never fully adopted the Rococo style, Neoclassicism was a natural development from the Palladian revival of the first half of the century. The floor plans of existing Palladian houses adapted well to Neoclassical layouts and decoration (which was fortunate, since few Neoclassical houses were built). The fundamental difference between Palladian style and Neoclassical style was that Neoclassicism was based on direct observation of Greek and Roman architecture, whereas its predecessor was based on interpretations by intermediaries (Palladio and the Roman architect Vitruvius, whose writings Palladio had studied).

INFLUENCES

Robert Adam dominated the Neoclassical period during the late 18th century. The Tapestry Room at Osterley Park House, West London, was designed by Adam around the Gobelin tapestries on the walls. The pull-up curtains are among the earliest still surviving.

The most influential architect of the time was the Scottish architect Robert Adam. He had been greatly inspired by his studies in art and architecture in France and Italy, and part of his skill was in developing original ideas from the old styles. He was an interior designer as well as an architect; indeed, because there were few major building projects at the time, most of his work was refurbishment of existing buildings.

Adam introduced a new lightness and elegance into interiors. Syon House, Osterley Park, Kenwood House and Harewood House were some of the great mansions he worked on.

Another great British Neoclassical architect, though not as fashionable as Adam, was William Chambers, who designed Somerset House in London. James Wyatt and Henry Holland were also important architects of the period, although somewhat later than Adam and Chambers. They used Neoclassical ornament more sparingly than Adam, but neither ever quite achieved such fully integrated schemes. Wyatt worked on a variety of projects, from church interiors and large Gothick houses such as Fonthill Abbey and Sheffield Park, to the magnificent Classical Heveningham Hall in Suffolk. Holland worked very much in the French style for his francophile patrons, importing French furniture and furnishings. One of his most famous projects was the interior of Carlton House, the Prince of Wales's London residence.

The spending power of the new English middle classes, who had grown wealthy from the new mechanization of industry and the development of trade, made them an influential group. Like the aristocracy, they understood the need for fashion one-upmanship, and all over the country delightful small houses were commissioned from local builders. Although the Classical look was much favoured, the Gothick and chinoiserie styles still thrived.

In France the late 18th century was a period devoted to comfort, lavish trimmings and graceful drapery. Even before Louis XVI began

Below: The late 18th century drapery in these alcoves in the Palais Royal is typical of what was known as the Grand Style. The curtains were intended to soften the architecture and were caught back in two or three different places. They are topped with a shaped, stiffened, tasselled pelmet.

Opposite: The Library at Osterley Park House. This is another room designed by Robert Adam, featuring early pull-up curtains and an Adam plasterwork ceiling. He brought a new lightness and elegance to interiors, emphasizing decoration rather than architectural feature

Élévation en face des croisées du Sallon au premier etage des nouveaux appartements du Palais Royal.

his reign in 1774 there had been a reaction against Rococo, and a revival of interest in Classicism. Louis XVI and his wife, Marie Antoinette, encouraged the Neoclassical style (known as Louis Seize style, after the King), and prior to the Revolution the court and Parisian society lived a life of great luxury and elegance. As Paris was the centre for the style, it had a high concentration of superb craftsmen.

Jacques-Ange Gabriel was one of the leading Neoclassical architects and interior designers in France, where the style appealed to the academic nature of the French. His early work had been in the Rococo style, but the École Militaire, and the twin buildings on the north side of the Place de la Concorde, show how well he had adapted to Neoclassicism. Possibly his greatest work was the Petit Trianon which, though small, was in perfect scale and harmony. The main rooms were rectangular and decorated in soft grey or white while the wall panelling and mirror frames were arched and the mouldings Classical. This style was widely copied and "small" was regarded as desirable in interiors. The magnificent fabric designs of Philippe de Lasalle and the restrained and formal decoration of Richard de Lalonde were also important influences during Louis XVI's reign.

As the Revolution approached, Neoclassical motifs developed a sinister symbolism of intent. The arts were increasingly inspired by antiquity, and arts and sciences were encouraged. The Directoire style which developed from the Louis Seize style at the end of the century was altogether a more austere and Classical adaptation of Greek and Roman art. The cabinet maker Georges Jacob and the painter Jacques Louis David were considerable influences of the period. Interior decoration became much plainer, characterized by flat-toned plastered walls or fabric hangings with Classical borders.

Despite a long reign of peace in 18th-century Italy, there was little change of style. The palatial splendour of the Baroque was still much favoured, appearing rather out of date against the rest of Europe. Here, too, the professional and middle classes were paying more attention to their homes and becoming more influential in architecture and interiors. It is ironic that Rome, which provided such inspiration for the whole Neoclassical period, should not have produced one notable public building of its own in the style. Nevertheless, the late 18th century Italian architect, designer and engraver, Piranesi, helped to redress the balance. His innumerable etchings of ancient Rome and his designs for furniture, mostly in the Neoclassical style, had a far-reaching influence.

Germany was still made up of numerous territories under princely rule. Vienna, the capital of the Habsburg territories and the Holy Roman Empire, was the emperors' official residence and the focal point of the arts. The Rococo was already firmly established there. However, once the Neoclassical style finally took hold, a number of

In clothing fashions too there was a reaction against the excesses of the Rococo style. Hoops for skirts decreased in size and were then replaced by pads, first on the hips and then at the back, giving a bustled appearance. Women's clothes in particular progressed towards a new simplicity.

Curtain treatments became lighter in the late 18th century, and graceful drapery, in which the fabric appeared to flow in one unbroken piece, was particularly fashionable.

A typical Gustavian interior. The stylized drapery above the window is still seen all over Scandinavia, sometimes teamed with slender muslin curtains.

splendidly severe public buildings were erected in the Greek Neoclassical style. Nevertheless, it was never favoured to the same extent in Germany as elsewhere. The only German Neoclassical designer to have any international influence was the furniture designer David Roentgen, the greatest German furniture maker and probably the most successful of all 18th century furniture designers.

There had been great similarities between Holland and England in the development of their interior styles. The future King Charles II of England spent some of his years of exile in Holland in the 17th century, and William III, who ruled Britain and Ireland with his wife Mary at the end of that century, was Dutch. Furthermore, both countries had benefited from the skills of Huguenot craftsmen who took refuge there late in the 17th century, spreading the sophisticated French taste. By the late 18th century, such was the popularity of French and English furniture that Holland in 1771 banned the importation of any furniture from abroad. This encouraged the Dutch cabinet-makers to experiment with the new Classical style.

Norway and Sweden were much influenced by Holland, not only through the large number of Dutch craftsmen working in Scandinavia but also through seagoing trade. Norway had been the main supplier of timber for the rebuilding of London after the Great Fire in the previous century, and Sweden also exported timber and iron ore. This was the start of much seagoing trade between Scandinavia and England and, as a result of their links with Holland and England, the two countries develped an "Anglo-Dutch style" of interior decoration. By the mid 18th century, the Danish and Swedish courts had adopted the French style, which gradually filtered down to the middle classes towards the end of the century. The Rococo style was particularly influential in Sweden because the court architect was Paris-trained.

The Swedes, however, brought their inimitably fresh approach to bear on all these various influences, resulting in the Gustavian style. This Neoclassical style emerged in the last quarter of the 18th century during the reign of Sweden's Gustave III, a brilliant and charismatic figure who made the Swedish court a northern Versailles. Gustavian style was characterized by a preference for symmetry and straight lines, a cool, understated elegance and more restrained ornamentation than in the quarter-century before, when the Rococo had been fashionable in Sweden. Painted furniture had been all the rage in Sweden since the middle of the century, but during the Gustavian period cooler, paler colours, such as straw yellow, pearl grey and muted blue, were favoured. The pieces were usually gessoed before being painted, for a smoother, more refined surface. Chairs, which were straight-legged, were painted *en suite* with the décor, in particular the panelling against which they were ranged.

Neoclassicism did not reach America until the late 1780s, after the War of Independence. The period prior to this is known broadly as the Colonial period (though within that there are distinct style-periods, such as Pilgrim Century). The period from when the new Federal Government was established, 1789, until the 1820s is called the Federal period. Many of the leaders of the new republic, particularly Thomas Jefferson, identified with the republican civilizations of Periclean Greece and Augustan Rome. Jefferson even draughted the Declaration of Independence on a writing box that was one of the first Neoclassical pieces to be found in America.

Neoclassicism dominated the Federal period, largely as a result of the influence of Robert Adam and the furniture pattern books of Hepplewhite and Sheraton. These books were particularly valuable because they scaled down Adam's palatial designs to a more popular and practical level. Hepplewhite's and Sheraton's designs were freely adapted for the American market, with many regional variations, particularly in decoration. There was much use of Neoclassical motifs, as well as the eagle, the bird chosen for the Great Seal of the United States (and also the symbol of the ancient Roman Republic). As in England, the style was characterized by refined proportion and ordered symmetry, clean lines and uncomplicated curves.

Although Neoclassicism had taken over from Rococo in Europe in

the 1760s, Rococo was just becoming familiar in America at that time. The period from around 1760 to 1785 (i.e. at the end of the Colonial period) is generally known as the Chippendale period. Here, too, it was furniture pattern books – Chippendale's *Director* (see page 53) and its rivals – that were largely responsible, along with imported English furniture, in this case English Rococo, with which Chippendale's name is synonymous.

In the late 18th century, lifestyles were becoming more relaxed, and comfort had become a priority in interior furnishings.

LIFESTYLE

In the second half of the 18th century there was a growing sophistication and a preoccupation with fashion. Technical advances increased people's desire for innovation, and the wealth was available to pay for constant change. In 1766 Horace Walpole wrote, "No fashion is meant to last longer than a lover." It was not just the aristocracy who had money to spend at this time; the authors and innovators of the time had to consider a much wider public. There were more engravings and colour plates available, and the arts thrived. The period had an elegant front – in Britain, for example, there were the plays of Sheridan and the paintings of Gainsborough and Reynolds – but violence stemming from social repression and poor living conditions simmered beneath the surface and there were politically inspired riots. Towards the end of the century, however, streets were noticeably cleaner and street lighting was improved.

Comfort became increasingly important. The French were finally

Until the French Revolution, the Parisian firm of Réveillon produced remarkable block-printed wallpapers imitating Pompeian paintings. This arabesque panel is typical of Réveillon's work.

copying the English idea of keeping the bedroom as a private place rather than a room of reception. The English in turn started to adopt the French concept of a dining-room, though it was to be reserved almost exclusively for special guests.

By the 1770s more attention was paid to rooms for entertaining people. Until then, furniture had generally been placed around the edge of the room when not in use. This was to enhance the architecture and, particularly in formal rooms such as the salon, to keep the centre of the floor for socializing. However, it was starting to become fashionable to place furniture around the floor and near the fireplace instead. By 1780 it was essential for every sofa to have a table standing permanently in front of it. Large armchairs were designed to blend with the décor of a particular room. Whereas in the earlier part of the century they were expected not to be tampered with or moved out of position, this was no longer the case. It was now widely believed that more informal seating layouts were the best way to promote sparkling conversation.

In London houses the vogue was for the wife's bedroom to be placed above her husband's and linked by a private staircase. The country bedroom would most probably have two dressing-rooms. The wife's dressing-room was usually furnished like a sitting-room with a canopied sofa bed, and here she might spend part of her day and receive her friends.

A distinctive feature of fashionable bedrooms, in both England and on the Continent, was the exquisite hand-painted Chinese paper that had become the vogue in the 1740s. Paint effects such as *trompe l'oeil*, marbling and graining were also much used in Neoclassical interiors, as well as wallpapers simulating marble, stucco and architectural features, and papers by the French firm of Réveillon. Generally regarded as the most artistic wallpapers ever produced, these were block-printed and featured Classical motifs in imitation of Pompeian paintings. Other wall treatments included papering with stripes and geometric motifs, and painting and decorating with a border. Grand rooms were still sometimes hung with damask, and Adam designed some rooms around Gobelin tapestries.

Classical motifs were also much used by Robert Adam on furniture, ceilings and walls, in the form of painted decoration and plasterwork. (He even invented a type of composition that allowed stick-on mouldings to be mass-produced.) Because of Adam this sort of decorative detail became important in Neoclassical interiors, making architectural features less dominant than previously. In many of his rooms, the main feature was the ceiling, the entire surface of which was decorated. Adam, like other Neoclassical architects, designed detailed schemes for interiors that encompassed every aspect, including mouldings on walls and ceilings, intricate colour schemes, carpet designs and specially designed furniture and mirrors. As a result, interiors were more coordinated than ever before. Another characteristic of Adam's style was elliptical or semi-circular rooms, with curved niches and arches.

Hand-knotted carpets were available at this time from Axminster and Moorfields, but from the 1760s strips of Brussels carpet (with a looped wool pile) and flat carpeting, woven by Kidderminster and by Wilton, were joined to cover large areas, and then surrounded by a complementary border. Canvas floor cloths painted with mosaic patterns were also very common, as were painted floors.

Print rooms – dressing-rooms or studies decorated with monochrome engravings pasted on the walls – also appeared during this period. The engravings were framed by engraved borders "hung" from *trompe l'oeil* paper bows, cords, chains and nails also pasted onto the walls. Paper swags, festoons and other Neoclassical ornament linked the engravings and were used as fillers among them. The walls were painted buff, grey, yellow, blue, green or pink to provide a plain background for the prints.

Furniture and Upholstery

Much of the furniture of the period was painted in matt colours. Of the unpainted furniture, satinwood was the most popular wood (except in the dining-room, where mahogany was preferred) and was often inlaid. Neoclassical furniture was generally simple and delicate, with straight legs. Although Chippendale designed some fine Neoclassical pieces, his name is associated with English Rococo, and it is Hepplewhite and Sheraton who are more closely linked to Neoclassicism. Their furniture pattern-books were highly influential.

Great advances were made in upholstery techniques at this time, with comfort a priority. These included air-filled mattresses and spring-cushioning. Seats were padded with a firm, resilient stuffing. In France the upholstery had a domed, stuffed shape whereas English work had a squarer profile produced by tufting. Squab cushions were sometimes used to soften cane dining chairs. Chairs were still covered with expensive materials *en suite* with the rest of the room and were therefore protected with loose covers. It was regarded as quite acceptable to sit on a chair even when this outer layer was in place, but the extra covers were usually removed for special occasions. In keeping with the Classical style, square rather than round lines were fashionable. Even bolsters became square.

A fashionable innovation towards the end of the century was to imitate the Turkish style of low seating. Sheraton set his behind columns. The seating only measured just over 30 centimetres (one foot) to the top of the cushions, and the supporting frame was beech webbed with canvas. Above the seating the whole height of the wall from cushion to cornice had a fixed deal frame which was covered first

OVERLEAF:
A successful blend of Neoclassical and modern, combining the elegance of late 18th century style window treatments, architectural features and Greek and Roman ornament with the simplicity of classic modern pieces.

with canvas, then the decorative fabric and then given a final flourish of swags at the top.

In France just before the Revolution there was a vogue for draping chairs and sofas with festoons, fringes and tassels.

Colours

Robert Adam introduced the idea of a richly coloured background – on either walls or ceiling – with delicate plasterwork details picked out in white or a strong colour, and this technique filtered through to the simplest homes. Colour played a very important part in Adam's designs. His palette included pale and medium green, lilac, apricot and opal tints and a stronger range of blues, greens and terracotta. Where it is possible to view Adam's original designs (in the British Museum), the colours can be seen in their full strength because they have not been exposed to sunlight; they are surprisingly strong and brilliant.

This applies not only to Robert Adam's palette. The colours we have come to associate with the past are actually only pale versions of the originals because sunlight, the linseed oil used in paints, and other factors have caused them to fade and yellow. In recent years, much research has been done into the field of historic colour. Modern techniques such as carbon dating allow particles of fabric, paint or paper to be analysed so that experts can then work out a suitable formula to reproduce them in their original colour(s). This means that if a designer working on a conservation project is lucky enough to find an original fragment of fabric or wall covering, it can be recreated accurately. The result is often something of a shock: the copies of the originals may seem strong and brash to our eyes.

Neoclassical English interiors featured Roman-inspired colour schemes (i.e. those that were supposed to have been advocated by the ancients), which were richer than the colours that had been used in Palladian-revival interiors. A more vivid palette was evident, including lilac, pink, bright blues and greens, strong yellow, and terracotta. The terracotta shade was based on the reds on antique Greek vases, which at the time were thought to be Etruscan. So-called "Etruscan rooms" had become fashionable, in which Classical motifs were picked out in terracotta and black.

In France, too, the Classical influence could be seen in the popularity of this same terracotta. There was also a cooler range of colours such as pale grey, blue, green, white and gold, during the time of Louis XVI. Directoire style featured a patriotic palette of red, white and blue, as well as deep green, violet, white and gold. Black and ivory on red, and light blue on dark blue, were typical combinations. A magnificent "Federation-style" bed of the period had violet, red and white silk swags around the corona, sky-blue taffeta curtains lined with red, a sky-blue damask counterpane and a white silk undercover with red drapery ornamented with a white geometric pattern.

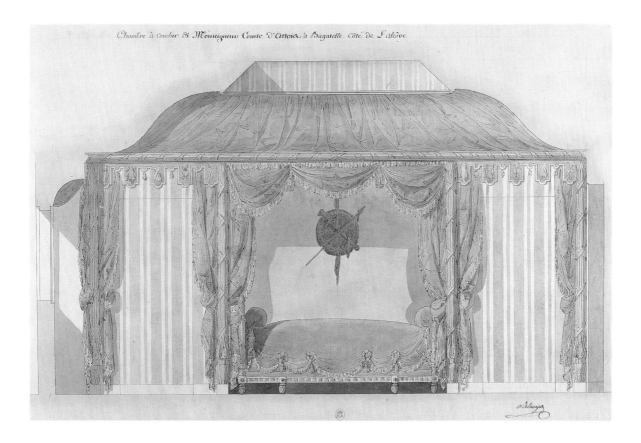

Chambre à coucher de Monsigneur Comte d'Artois à Bagatelle. Côté de l'Alcôve.

There were other colour influences in the second half of the 18th century, such as the beautiful colours of Wedgwood pottery, with the wide range of blues that was their trademark as well as lilac, red, green, brown and cane yellow. The Aubusson and Gobelins tapestry factories were flourishing, with Gobelins specializing in clear, warm shades, while Aubusson worked with red and green backgrounds and a blue known as "Boucher" from the artist's work.

America had its own unique range of colours at this time, including Salem white, Newport yellow, Virginia and Charleston green, Windsor gold and "cupboard red", so-called because the corner cabinet always revealed this colour. The Shaker movement, founded in 1774, produced simple furniture in soft red, blue, green and yellow.

By the end of the century, the manufacture of ready-mixed paints had begun. These were in the flat, matt tones that had been in general use since around 1740. The aspect of a room was now taken into account when choosing a colour scheme; cool colours were recommended for south-facing rooms and warmer tones for those facing north.

American Interiors

In America from the middle of the century, many cabinet makers took their inspiration from Chippendale's *Director* and rival pattern-books, but the Colonial furniture was fundamentally practical and there was a limited number of designs. Mahogany had by now replaced

Fashionably cool blues in a late 18th century design for a bedroom in a French château belonging to the Comte d'Artois, later Charles X of France.

walnut as the principal wood. Although the fashionable Rococo style was found in some wealthy homes, traditional country furniture was the norm. The widely differing nationalities of the settlers continued to give distinct regional styles.

Country houses were decorated with an eclectic mix of folk art, with wood floors often painted or stencilled, and rag rugs and patchwork brightening up the homes. Floors were also now sometimes covered with imported patterned rugs, but painted floor cloths were still widely used. The grandest homes had parquet flooring and imported carpets, curtains and bed hangings of silk damask, satin brocade, taffeta and cotton muslin. In the North, most of the walls were plastered; wood panelling was restricted to the chimneybreast and the alcoves or cupboards on either side. In the South, however, rooms were fully panelled. Softer, lighter colours were used for painting woodwork. Ceilings, now plastered, were often decorated in the Rococo style, though more simply than in England or France.

Fabrics in designs specifically for the growing American market were being produced by the late 18th century. This copperplate-printed toile, produced in Britain shortly after America's War of Independence, depicts George Washington, Benjamin Franklin, Liberty and the 13 states of the new republic.

During this period wealthy Southern planters and Eastern merchants built brick mansions in the Palladian revival style, and by the 1790s the Neoclassical style was well established. The new republic's third president, Thomas Jefferson, favoured the simplest Classical forms, and he used these for both the interior and the exterior of his own home, Monticello, which he designed himself and which had a great influence on American style of the period. Jefferson had developed many of his ideas from English architects. Elegant town houses were also built during the Federal period. An innovation of Federal houses was the dining-room, and new pieces of furniture were introduced for use in it, including the sideboard, extending tables and the lolling chair (an upholstered armchair with a high back with serpentine cresting, now also known as a Martha Washington chair).

A room from a country house near Philadelphia built in 1762. The mahogany furniture is in the Chippendale style, which was favoured in America then. As in England at the time, the upholstery is *en suite* with the handsome swagged silk damask curtains.

The increased amount of leisure time led to the development of the card table; when not in use, a pair of these would be positioned symmetrically along a wall as pier tables. (The card table is probably the piece of Federal furniture most available today.) Mahogany was still the preferred wood for furniture, though cherry, birch, walnut and maple were used in rural areas. Veneers were now increasingly available. Surfaces were decorated with inlaid motifs – cornucopias, garlands, baskets of fruit, etc. – and with strings of alternating wood tones.

Adam's influence was noticeable in Federal houses, but the decoration was simpler than in Britain. Wallpapers – including many with Classical motifs – were imported. (America's first indigenous wallpaper factory had been set up in 1765, in New York, but by the beginning of the 19th century there were still only a handful of U.S. printers manufacturing wallpaper.) "Classically inspired French" scenic papers (see page 114), which initially were hand-painted, were becoming highly sought-after, and some were produced in France specifically for the growing American market.

In the meantime, in the Southwest, a Hispanic tradition was developing, with simply furnished adobe houses, as this region was controlled by Spain into the 19th century.

CURTAINS AND DRAPERY

Neoclassicism resulted in formal yet opulent curtains and drapery, with a prevalence of Classical motifs in the decoration, as in other aspects of the interiors of the period. In France "the Grand Style" was conceived to soften the new severe Classical architecture. The range of fabrics available was much wider and trimmings were exquisite – an art form in themselves.

Beds and Bed Hangings

From the middle of the century, the designing of beds had passed from the upholsterer to the cabinet makers, carvers, gilders and painters, and so inevitably the hangings became of secondary importance. One of the most important features was now an elaborate cornice which often was repeated with the window curtains.

During the vogue for chinoiserie, windows and beds were often hung *en suite* with Chinese silk or embroidered fabrics featuring Oriental motifs. Towards the end of the century in France, beds were frequently adorned with divinities from the banks of the Nile.

Eighteenth-century America had followed the same fashions in beds and their hangings as Europe. As the century advanced, curtains were shortened or could be drawn up on a cord system in order to allow the increasingly ornate carving on the bedposts to be seen. As in Europe,

Traditional country furniture and unsophisticated fabrics were the norm in the less wealthy Colonial American homes.

87

there was generally a lighter look to hangings; often in silk or block-printed cottons with patterns of birds or flowers, they had an Oriental feel and were made in a wide range of colours, including red, purple, brown, blue, yellow and a green made from combining blue and yellow.

Copperplate-printed toiles (see page 96) were also in use from 1760. Velvet hangings with gold fringings were still a popular choice, and some of the most beautiful American beds were ornamented with crewel embroidery. Scalloped bed valances were fashionable. Some bed curtains pulled up on a cord-and-ring system to give a type of double festoon.

A 17th century Swedish home with charming late 18th-century furnishings. The painted decoration of the ceiling contrasts satisfyingly with the cool linden green of the draped bed.

Bed covers were designed to keep the occupant warm in cold, draughty rooms. Wool blankets with embroidered corners, followed by up to five quilts and then a richly decorated counterpane with a protective coverlet were on top of the sleeper, while the curtains around the frame of the bed helped to retain the heat.

In the 1790s Thomas Sheraton designed a number of unusual and delightful beds. One example was the charming curved-ended bed, set sofa-like in an alcove, on a raised dais, the outline softened by swags with tasselled ends. The bed curtains fell from a central corona and were caught back on cloak pins at each end of the bed.

Sheraton's "Summer Bed in a Compartment" comprised two single beds which had swagged valances and elegant fitted bedcovers bearing Neoclassical motifs, and which were covered by a large swagged tester

Above: With the vogue for lighter bed drapery, attention was focused on the bed posts themselves. These are designs by Chippendale.

supported by four posts. The beds themselves were divided by an attractive arch, also swagged and tasselled.

Of an "Elliptic bed for a single lady", Sheraton wrote, "As fancifulness seems more peculiar to the taste of females I have therefore assigned the use of this bed for a single lady though it will equally accommodate a single gentleman! The elliptic shape of the frame of this bed contracts its width at each end considerably on which account it will not admit of more than one person." The whole bed was surmounted by a domed tester; the drapery was tacked to the cornice, and the curtains were raised and lowered on pulleys located under the tester and tied to the pillars with cords.

Sheraton's Duchesse beds were generally lighter and more informal in style than their French counterparts, the *lits à la duchesse.* The

In this bedroom decorated by Stanley Falconer of Colefax and Fowler, the pretty green leaf chintz has been contrast-bound at its gathered top edge and finished with a two-tone linen fan edging at the bottom. The chinoiserie wallpaper and light bed treatment are consistent with the late 18th century style.

bedheads were formed like the back of a chair and the full tester was attached to the wall, with the drapery falling in swags and tails to the floor. The centre of the tester was usually dressed with plumes and the frame swagged. It was still fashionable for state beds to be heavily draped and their decoration very symbolic.

Another innovation was a type of bed for servants; pulley-operated, it descended from the wall.

In Sweden a major innovation of the period was the Gustavian bed, a forerunner of the modern sofa-bed. With its carved and painted wooden panels, it looked like a cross between a long, narrow sofa and a bateau bed. Although it had a slightly formal look, it was nevertheless found even in fairly humble households.

French drapery in the latter part of the 18th century was elegant and restrained and was designed as an integral part of the scheme. Complex borders were often an important part of the design.

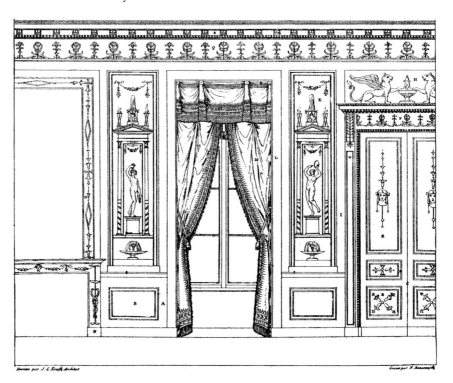

Windows

As the century advanced, the glazing bars of sash windows became more and more delicate and the most important feature of the window. Britain's Building Act of 1774 required that sash boxes be almost completely hidden, which emphasized the slender lines of these late-Georgian windows. The frame was of less importance, but the use of stone surrounds gave some weight and definition to the frame.

The tallest sash windows tended to be on the ground floor and the first floor, where the main apartments were located. The inclusion of a *piano nobile* with taller windows, introduced with the Palladian revival (see page 53), was commonplace in even fairly modest homes by the end of the century. First-floor drawing-room window sills were often at floor level and opened onto a balcony, and by the 1780s the sashes

of these windows had been replaced by French doors to give easy access to the balcony (or garden if on the ground floor).

By the end of the century there were variations on sashes, such as round-headed or elliptical-headed window openings with arched or rectangular sash frames.

The bay or bow window was popular from the mid 18th century. It was often made up of three separate windows, sometimes all three of them working sash windows. In the last quarter of the century, elliptical and canted bays were increasingly used.

Symmetry was important in Neoclassical architecture, so sometimes "blind" windows (plain recesses in the masonry or even fake sashes) were inserted to maintain visual balance when a real window would have been impossible.

An elaborate pennant-style window treatment by John Fowler. The red lining of the curtains is also visible on the centre choux and on the outer tails. At the outside edge the headings are held by bows. This treatment has a distinct Neoclassical quality.

One of Chippendale's carved wooden curtain cornices, which he designed in the early 1760s. These cornices still had quite a strong Rococo feel even though they were combined with more Classical drapery, as Neoclassicism had begun to take over from the Rococo only a few years before.

Curtains

In late 18th-century England, simple, straight-hung curtains were still widely used, often tacked straight onto the window frame. The new fuller pull-ups were also popular and were almost always topped with a pelmet cornice, which in the grander houses would be carved and gilded. The carved wooden cornices of Thomas Chippendale and Thomas Sheraton were a feature of the period. These were varied and charming. They could be carved, carved and gilded or carved and japanned, and were frequently curved at the end. Ornamentation included scrolls, leaves, swags of leaves, vases of fruit and flowers, and star and flower shapes.

A major innovation was the introduction of a full cord-and-pulley system (often called French rods) to open and close draw-curtains with minimum inconvenience and damage to the curtain fabric. The use of an overlap where the curtains met in the centre gave a much better finish.

By the 1780s it was fashionable for French-rod curtains to have draperies or pelmets attached above the window to hide the workings, and the operating cords often had decorative tasselled ends.

Muslin subcurtains were frequently installed to protect furnishings from sunlight. Green-painted spring roller blinds could be used in conjunction with straight or drapery curtains. Screens reminiscent of sashes were sometimes fitted to the bottom half of the window and painted green to give privacy.

Reefed curtains, also called Italian-strung curtains, which pulled up and apart by means of diagonally strung cords, while the actual heading remained fixed, were in vogue. These could be made so that they pulled up in two pieces, forming swags and tails, and the curtains were then caught back at dado height to prevent them from trailing on the floor. The cutting of these drapery curtains was highly subtle, the combinations of fabrics used eye-catching and the trimmings exquisite.

Drapery was the most fashionable type of curtaining in the Neoclassical period. Simple drapery consisted of several separate pieces put together to give the appearance of one flowing piece. There was usually one or more swags to go at each end with the joins disguised by some sort of trimming. It was all constructed so that each pleat of the drapery would follow around gracefully from one side to the other without breaking the continuity of the fold or drawing on the adjoining pleats.

This was particularly awkward where the swags met over a rod or pole and failed to conceal the seams. Careful binding was used to overcome the problem. Swags and tails often had contrasting lining such as crimson velvet against oyster silk. To soften the outlines of the window and diffuse the light, they were frequently combined with dress curtains, as opposed to full working curtains.

Irregular drapery was also used at this time, in which swags were attached at different heights, as on an arch. They gave a lighter, more airy feel than straight swags. Swags were sometimes used as a supplementary decoration to a cornice or pair of curtains. They would appear to be attached but were in fact laid over the curtains and, like the curtains, were attached to the cornice. A large cord and tassel would complete the illusion.

In the 1790s Sheraton designed light, elegant curtains, caught back with rope tie-backs, ornamented with large rosettes and topped with a cornice and valance which had been softened with the attachment of swags and mini-tails. For the Chinese drawing-room of the Prince of Wales, Sheraton designed Gothick-style pelmets with narrow "Pagoda"-style cornices, the rich figured satin-bordered curtains tied back three-quarters of the way down.

Draperies in France in the second half of the 18th century were light and fanciful, often in pale tones of grey and lilac. During the reign of Louis XVI (1774–1792) the supple and elegant draped curtains, in what was often referred to as "the Grand Style", were in perfect harmony with the rather discreet style of the period. Window pelmets were often castellated and combined with Italian-style curtains and under-curtains. Swags, where they were used, were shallow and regular. There was a wide variety of curtain ornamentation, including wreaths, tassels, sprays of leaves, bows, swags of greenery and feathers. Many designs were Classically inspired.

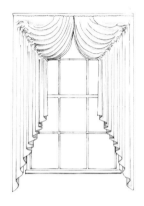

With Italian-strung, or reefed, curtains, the heading remains stationary and the curtains pull up to the sides like theatre curtains to allow the maximum amount of light into the room.

A selection of late 18th century cornices designed to complement the Neoclassical styles of curtain.

By 1785 French draperies were fuller but remained symmetrical. It was still fashionable to soften the architecture with fabric. Pelmets were softened with swags and could be enlivened with a decoration of tapestry sometimes applied in a separate rosette in the centre of the pelmet. Where borders were used on the walls, these were often continued on the curtains and pelmet. Pelmets and tie-backs were decorated with borders, braids and ribbons, bows and tassels.

During the Revolutionary period symmetry began to be abandoned, but the general aspect was well balanced and without opulence, though it could appear rather hard-edged.

In Italy Venetian blinds were now in use and by 1760 these had reached England. In France they were known as *jalousie à la persienne*. Though versatile in application, they were fragile to handle as the horizontal laths tended to come away from the supporting tapes very easily.

In America window curtains were fairly rare before the Revolution due to the huge expense of the fabric. The English style was dominant and wealthy colonists could order their furnishings from London to their specification or from English upholsterers who had settled in the colonies and set themselves up in business. They could take ideas from the pattern-books such as Chippendale's *Director*, which suggested

These windows have been treated in an identical and dramatic way, with the single curtains caught back to one side with ropes and tassels in two places. The use of two tie-backs is reminiscent of the Grand Style favoured in France towards the end of the 18th century.

suitable fabrics and styles on a room-by-room basis, and also from the homes of the English Royal Governors. As in Europe, the quality of the interior hangings of a home gave status to its owner but silk was not used so often in America because of the cost of importing it. (The first American silk factory was not built until 1810.) Instead, substitutes would be silk/wool mixes and worsted woollens, which could be specially treated (with heavy weights) to resemble glossy silks.

Fabrics

One of Robert Adam's innovations was the practice of using window and upholstery fabrics that were either the same or similar in colour. This fashion continued into the 19th century.

The British silk industry was at its height now, with painted silks imported from China and silk damasks and brocades made in England. More sophisticated looms were developed in the second half of the century which could produce complex weaves, giving impetus to the whole industry.

Lyons still produced magnificent fabrics. For Marie Antoinette's bed they created a wonderful satin with a white ground covered with a grand design of ribbons, colonnades, sprays of foliage, garlands of foliage, garlands of flowers and branches of oak and laurel. As the Revolution approached, there was a return to Classical designs including acanthus, medallions, lozenges, festoons and vases.

Another development at this time was copperplate printing, which changed the appearance of cotton textiles and made larger repeats and better definition possible. This method was used for the first toile, which was actually printed in Ireland in 1752. It was not until 1770 that the famous factory at Jouy, which remains synonymous with toiles to this day, began printing them. Printed in single colours (blue, red, violet or sepia) using vegetable dyes on an off-white ground of undyed calico, the toiles featured finely etched Neoclassical designs (rustic scenes, ancient buildings, mythological subjects, events of the time, etc.). They were used flat as wall panels so that the detail of the picture could be seen. The soft toile effect was achieved by repeatedly washing and bleaching the fabric and afterwards passing it through rollers.

Towards the end of the century ikats from the Far East in silk or cotton depicting symbolic patterns of everyday life began to be imported. Muslin, which had come exclusively from India until this time, was now imported from Switzerland. Glazed chintz was introduced too.

Kashmiri shawls imported by the East India Company from India were immediately popular but they were very scarce and very expensive so British craftsmen (mainly at Spitalfields in London, and Norwich) started to copy them. England also imported checked and striped cottons from India. French manufacturers commissioned leading artists to design similar patterns to those of Kashmir but more in keeping with European taste. From the 1780s Paisley in Scotland became the main centre for producing these Kashmir-inspired designs, giving its name to the new "paisley" patterns.

Most fabrics carried motifs such as bouquets, ribbons, wreaths, garlands or birds. Oriental fabrics and chinoiserie generally remained popular. Embroidered textiles were still much in use, and in England a wool-and-goathair mix, known as camlet, was highly sought after.

Loose covers in simple checked cotton or linen gingham, or sometimes printed cotton or chintz, were widely used to protect furniture upholstered in expensive fabrics. It was the Swedes, however, who recognized the potential of these fabrics, using brightly checked cotton or linen chair seats and bed hangings to complement much of their Gustavian painted wooden furniture.

By the end of the century, America's homespun linen and wool weaves had been largely replaced by imported printed cottons and chintz in the "Indian taste" and silk brocades and damasks. At around this time, cotton became an important crop there, and after Eli Whitney's invention of the cotton gin speeded up the process of separating the fibre from the seeds, the country's cotton-spinning industry flourished.

Trimmings

There was an abundance of ornamentation in the 18th century. Most trimmings of this period were made of silk; violet, yellow and brown were fashionable colours. Braids were decorated with stylized floral designs or were bobbled or decorated with appliquéd bows, rosettes or butterfly shapes. Picot or gimp braids served as a top for plain, fluffy, spiral or bullion fringes, some of which were extra-long and carried appliquéd decoration. An alternative heading was a delicate trellis of lace.

Mid-18th century tassels tended to have smaller, arrow-shaped or rectangular heads, and the fringed skirts of the tassels were proportionately shorter too. A trimming of appliquéd bows on the skirt as well as the head was a popular decoration. By the end of the century, tassels were smaller and had plaited tops. The skirt could be ornamented with fabric-covered wooden shapes and trimmed with bobbles at top and base.

Macaroons were circular trimmings used to give definition on tie-backs or in conjunction with tassels. They would be satin-covered and braid-trimmed, and carry appliqué work or bouclé knots. Tie-backs too were satin-covered and tasselled and frequently braid-edged, encrusted and appliquéd.

5

THE EARLY 19TH CENTURY

Regency and Empire Styles

Early 19th century European and American homes were still essentially Neoclassical, but with certain differences from the 18th century versions. In England, this late-Neoclassical style came to be known as Regency style, after the period 1811–1820 when the Prince of Wales (later George IV) was Regent. The style-period actually covers the half-century or so from around 1790 to about 1840.

In much of continental Europe the late-Neoclassical style became known as Empire, after France's First Empire (1804–1814). Here, too, the style-period started earlier, beginning in France in the 1790s. From France, Empire style spread to Holland, Germany, Scandinavia, Italy and Spain, and it was also taken up by furniture makers in America. After about 1814, when Napoleon was forced to abdicate and Louis XVIII became king of France (the beginning of the so-called Restauration period), the Empire style gradually declined in importance.

Underlying both the Regency and the Empire styles was an appreciation of Classicism in a purer, simpler form, with less emphasis on fussy decoration than in Robert Adam's interiors. Ancient Greece and Egypt were the main sources of inspiration. And whereas 18th century Neoclassicism had mainly been confined to the aristocracy, these new styles reached a much wider audience in a Europe that was undergoing a series of social changes.

INFLUENCES

In France trade and industry were booming, and much more middle-class housing was being built. Smaller rooms were fashionable, and so furniture and decorative objects had to be scaled down accordingly. After Napoleon's Nile Campaign, his prestige was high. An admirer of the art of Imperial Rome (not least because he liked to associate himself with the splendours of the Roman Empire), Napoleon went to great lengths to encourage the arts, setting an example in patronage which was followed by the new rich. Although the Louis Seize style and

The Prince of Wales was a serious patron of design and decoration and took a great interest in the interiors of his royal residences. Here, in the magnificent Crimson Drawing Room of Carlton House, the walls and windows are heavily swagged.

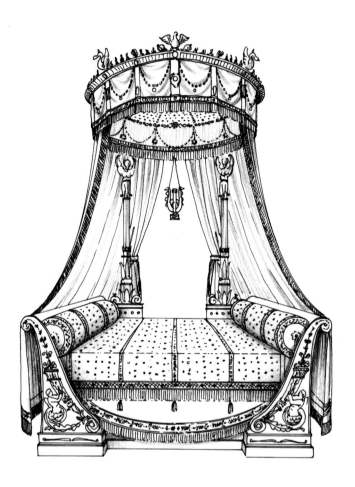

The influential French designers, Percier and Fontaine, designed this luxurious bed for the Empress Josephine at Malmaison. Built by the leading furniture-maker Jacob-Desmalter, it was exotically carved, and gilded, the walls tented and the ceiling painted.

18th century Neoclassicism still lingered on, Classicism was now revived in its original purity.

The architects Percier and Fontaine, who had studied the originals in Italy, were possibly the greatest exponents of Classicism and the Empire style's most important designers. During the Directoire (see page 72) they had worked on the restoration of the Royal Palaces, and they subsequently redesigned the Empress Josephine's Château de Malmaison. Their magnificently integrated work there was copied all over Europe. The Malmaison interiors varied hugely, from the elegant and restrained music room to the exotic bedroom of the Empress with its gilded bed, tenting and painted ceiling. After their work at Malmaison, Napoleon kept Percier and Fontaine fully occupied as architects, interior decorators and designers until his abdication. They believed furniture to be an important part of any interior and often worked with the great cabinet-maker Georges Jacob and later his son Jacob-Desmalter, the most celebrated furniture maker of the period. Percier and Fontaine's much acclaimed book *Recueil des Décorations Intérieurs* was influential throughout Europe. When it was first published (in serial form) in 1801, it contained in it virtually the entire

basis of the Empire style. (It also employed the term "interior decoration" for the first time.)

Napoleon liked to surround himself with all things military, and this resulted in *"le style héroique"*, featuring spear heads, campaign tents and the like. It has also been suggested that one of the factors behind Percier and Fontaine's use of so much fabric on walls and in tented effects at Malmaison was Napoleon's notorious impatience to get things done in a hurry, since this was a relatively quick way of creating an opulent effect. The fabric also muffled evidence of his outbursts of temper!

In England too it was a time of social change. The general feeling of unrest and the agitation against injustice led to political reform. The abolition of slavery in 1807 was a notable advance and it was believed that the Parliamentary Reform Bill averted the possibility of a revolution. In the early 1800s the new wealth was well spread around

Percier and Fontaine often used tented walls and ceilings in their Empire interiors, and these became fashionable in England when their designs were published there.

the country, and residential areas sprang up not only in London but in many other major cities. The Great English House was no longer what people aspired to, as smaller, more elegant manor houses and villas became fashionable. New building techniques using brick and stucco instead of Portland stone helped to keep prices down. Spas and seaside resorts were popular, and homes were planned for leisure and to maximize the feeling of light and space.

There was something of a reaction against the work of Robert Adam, and other architects moved into the limelight. Among these was John Nash, whose elegant Classical buildings, faced in stucco painted to look like Bath stone, were often the result of royal commissions, as in London's Regent's Park terraces. It was Nash who recreated Buckingham Palace from Buckingham House and who rebuilt Henry Holland's Brighton Pavilion in Oriental style. (The interior decoration at Brighton was largely the work of Frederick Crace, whose father, John C. Crace, had provided much of the furniture, and whose son, John G. Crace, went on to collaborate with A.W.N. Pugin on the interiors of London's Houses of Parliament. The family firm of Crace & Son was one of the most successful furniture-making and interior design firms of the 19th century.) Another architect of the period, Sir John Soane, was noted for his inventiveness and restrained symmetry, qualities that

In England the Assembly Rooms at Bristol and Bath were focal points of Regency society. An arch in the cloakroom in Clifton Assembly Rooms, Bristol, is decorated with swags caught back on rosettes over a deep valance.

Opposite: The Prince Regent commissioned Henry Holland to alter and extend Carlton House in the late 18th century. In the Circular Room the drapery softens and complements the architecture.

The boudoir, or small drawing room, in the designer Thomas Hope's country house, Deepdene, in Surrey. Hope's decorative sense was greatly influenced by his extensive travels, and the construction over the sofa is reminiscent of Percier's early designs.

were evident in his own homes at Lincoln's Inn Fields, London, and Pitshanger Manor in Ealing. The simple, refined decorative details he devised for his early houses were used in innumerable small Regency homes.

The French influence was evident in Regency style, as the Napoleonic Wars did not stop French and English designers and style-setters from visiting each other's countries between hostilities. Elements of both the Directoire style (see page 72) and the Empire style were apparent, and the introduction of Egyptian elements into English interiors was a direct result of the British navy's great victory over the French at the Battle of the Nile in 1798, when Nelson cut off Napoleon's army in Egypt. Thomas Sheraton's *Cabinet Dictionary* (1803) contained a number of designs celebrating Nelson's victories at sea. The British victory at Trafalgar in 1805 led to the "Trafalgar chair" with a cable-twist back rail and sabre legs. Napoleon's retreat from Russia prompted a wave of Russian eagles on English furniture, mirrors and silver. The work of Percier and Fontaine was influential in England at this time, too, particularly their tenting and draping. The Prince Regent, a major patron of the arts, favoured French styles combined with something of the exotic and dramatic. By the age of 21, he had already established this role when in 1783 he commissioned Henry Holland to alter and extend Carlton House in London, using Greco-Roman and Louis Seize themes.

There was, nevertheless, an underlying feeling of patriotism in England which led to a preference for the essential English styles, revivals of many of which began around the early part of the century (see Chapter 6). None of these revivals overshadowed Neoclassicism at this time, however.

Magazines were becoming increasingly available and, in England, Rudolph Ackermann produced his *Repository of Arts* magazine, which not only had magnificent curtain designs and room sets but also had real samples of fabric stuck to the pages and authoritative advice on interior decoration and furnishing. The *Repository* held strong views. It promoted decorating *en suite* and encouraged fringes and net worked in gold-coloured silk and firescreens with embossed gold borders. Symbolism and Classical reference were also encouraged. The text accompanying the window treatments was always enthusiastic, as in the following example. "Perhaps no furniture is more decorative and graceful than that of which draperies form a considerable part; the easy disposition of the lines composing their form and the harmonious combination of their colours, produced a charm that brought them into high repute." Once Napoleon was safely exiled in St. Helena after his defeat at Waterloo in 1815 by the Duke of Wellington, the magazine featured the work of Percier and Fontaine.

The furniture designer and patron of the arts, Thomas Hope, completed an incredibly lengthy eight-year Grand Tour and then produced his important book *Household Furniture and Decoration*, which had considerable influence on English furniture design. He had visited Turkey, Spain, Syria, Greece and Italy but favoured the Grecian ornament that was a feature of Regency interiors, as opposed to the Roman motifs beloved of Percier and Fontaine. In his furniture designs he copied ancient furniture more closely than practically anyone had previously. His own London house contained some startling interiors influenced by his extensive travels, and Deepdene, his Surrey home, was much admired.

Thomas Sheraton and George Smith, cabinet-makers and upholsterers, both wrote a number of influential books. Sheraton's last work was *The Cabinet-Maker, Upholsterer and General Artist's Encyclopaedia* (1804–1806), of which only 30 of the projected 125 parts were published. His books were widely used in the United States,

OVERLEAF:
A simple half-tester with swagged valance frames the bed in this charming Swedish bedroom. The bed and chairs are decorated *en suite*.

where the pieces were given their own individual and regional interpretations.

Germany, along with Central Europe and Scandinavia, had been left impoverished by Napoleon's blockade. Economy was therefore an important factor in interior decoration, and there the Empire style evolved into the simple, functional and affordable Biedermeier style, with its thick curtains and padded upholstery. Small-scale furniture was made for the smaller-scale rooms in woods such as cherry, pear and maple, sometimes with an ebony inlay. Upholstery was usually in bright reds or blues in plain woollen cloth.

In Scandinavia, the French influence was to the fore. English influence on interior styles and architecture gave way to the Empire style, which was succeeded by the Biedermeier style.

In Holland the Empire style held sway at the beginning of the century, and Biedermeier was its natural successor.

The more modest homes of the Italians were spartan at this time, but magnificent Empire interiors were created by specially imported French craftsmen for Napoleon's two brothers (the king of Naples and the prince of Carvino) and three sisters, all of whom lived in Italy. As it developed in Italy, the Empire style became heavier and over-elaborate.

Among Americans there was a growing desire for a national style. Although the work of Robert Adam was firmly established by 1800, they now preferred to interpret rather than just borrow ideas. The Federal style was the American version of Neoclassicism, and they gave their own look to Robert Adam's style and subsequently to both the Empire and the Regency styles. The flying, or free-standing, staircase in the entrance hall and curved architectural features were notable characteristics of the houses of the period. One of the principal architects of the time, apart from Thomas Jefferson, was Asher Benjamin, who wrote the influential *The Country Builder's Assistant* and *The American Builder's Companion*. The Americans took a more practical and frugal approach to their architecture and interiors, which often resulted in a pared-down and simplified adaptation of Continental trends. Nevertheless, the Empire style brought to America a more imposing style of decoration and furnishing, with heavier textiles. Lasting from around 1810 to 1820, the last part of the Federal period, American Empire style was inspired by Greek, Roman and Egyptian sources.

America looked towards France more than England for inspiration at this time. The people felt politically disposed to the French, following the War of 1812 and also because of France's support in the American War of Independence. Furthermore, French pattern books were available in America, as well as the English ones (of which at any rate Thomas Hope's and George Smith's were French-influenced). Other factors leading Americans to favour the French were the import

Elegant continuous drapery links the windows in Elizabeth of Bavaria's bedchamber in Tegernsee Castle. The Empire-style bed is placed sideways against the wall, and the bed curtains are caught back with cloakpins at either end. The other furniture is in the increasingly fashionable Biedermeier style.

of Louis XVI furniture by Franklin, Jefferson and Washington after the dispersal of French royal property in 1794, and the influx of French immigrants as a result of the French Revolution.

LIFESTYLE

In England the early 19th century was a time of great industrial development. Major cities were linked by canal, and steam was used to power mills and factories. The first steam carriages were seen on the roads. The increased mechanization and improvements in dye techniques resulted in more affordable textiles. Wallpapers could now be mass-produced, and the quality of plate glass was so much better that fewer glazing bars were needed.

Special machinery could produce finely detailed joinery and there were advances in the production of metal for building. Early forms of heating from steam or hot water piping appeared in private homes. There was gas lighting and the first ball-cock lavatory cisterns. Admiral Nelson was one of the very first to have *en suite* bathrooms installed in his home. Additional libraries were built and more newspapers and magazines became available. All this gave the country greater power abroad and more money to spend at home, and this new wealth was, to a large extent, transferred to bricks and mortar.

The way interiors were used started to change. The library, once a male preserve, became a room in which the whole family read and played games. This could be linked to a formal drawing-room (often now on the ground floor) by double doors, which were only opened on special occasions. It was fashionable for the French doors of the drawing-room to open directly onto the garden or terrace. Conservatories were introduced, and the flower garden returned to a position near the house, in keeping with the new rustic, romantic style. Breakfast rooms were in vogue, and the saloon was relegated to little more than a passage.

In Regency times the library became a place which the entire family could use for relaxation and recreation. This is the library at Cassiobury Park, Hertfordshire, a late 17th century room that was redecorated in Regency style by James Wyatt around 1800. The much greater degree of comfort is very apparent.

Mirrors were used a great deal to give the required feeling of light and space, and furniture was always arranged at angles. The couch was an important feature and actively encouraged reclining. Sofas were now placed not along the walls but at right angles to them or facing the fireplace, with a sofa table in front. Chairs were left permanently in the centre of the room rather than against the walls. A large pedestal table often had pride of place in the middle of the room. There was a new informality in lifestyle and manners – legs were crossed and hands kept in pockets!

The tented walls and ceilings that were fashionable in Empire France started to appear in England, in brocades, silks and chintzes. The French versions were usually in satin or cotton with symmetrical

patterns featuring, say, the Napoleonic bee or medallions, or they were in monochromatic toiles. Black borders unified them. Fabrics depicting scenes of campaigns in Egypt or Italy were also popular. Decorative paint finishes were fashionable again, along with sophisticated wallpapers such as flock, moiré and papers simulating decorative effects. Clouded ceilings were now very fashionable.

Fitted carpets were in general use. Persian carpets were much admired, and serge or baize druggets were used to protect good-quality carpets from dirt and general wear-and-tear. By this time interior decoration was being seen in the average home and was not just the province of the very rich.

Furniture and Upholstery

Empire-style furniture tended to be quite plain and heavy. Mahogany, rosewood and satinwood were popular initially, as they were in Regency England, but in France they became scarce because of the European blockade, so native woods (maple, beech, walnut, oak, fruitwoods) were increasingly used there. Sofas and chairs had square backs and were usually covered *en suite.* Arms were often in the form of winged sphinxes, and legs were sabre-shaped.

Fitted carpets were in use in Regency England, as can be seen in this watercolour of a dining room of circa 1818. The fringed swags over poles combined with paired curtains caught back in the distinctive, slightly ballooned shape are typical of the period, too. Blinds, to protect the furniture from the sun, are just visible beneath the curtains.

111

A modern interpretation of tenting gives an original effect over a staircase and landing.

Regency furniture was very elegant, particularly the chairs, which were usually low, with curved backs, brass inlay and sabre legs. They could either be upholstered or have caned seats with squab cushions. *Chaises longues* were popular, and the fashionable sofa was the Grecian couch, with roll-curved ends, bolster cushions and carved feet. In George Smith's *The Cabinet Maker and Upholsterer's Guide*, published in 1826, sofas already had stumpy turned legs. That same year saw the development of spiral-spring upholstery, which gave a deeper and springier stuffing and softer feel to the upholstery.

By 1830 striped cotton or linen upholstery and loose covers were much in evidence. Upholstery and sometimes even tables and sideboards were almost permanently protected by loose covers. It was fashionable for chairs and sofas to be upholstered in the same colour as the curtains. Rich chintzes were often used, with the main motif featured on the back of the chair. Leather was used for library and dining chairs, and satin and damask for sofas.

Colours

At the turn of the century, colours tended to be rather drab but by the time the Regency was firmly established in England, they had become vivid and daring, with a range that included cherry red, deep

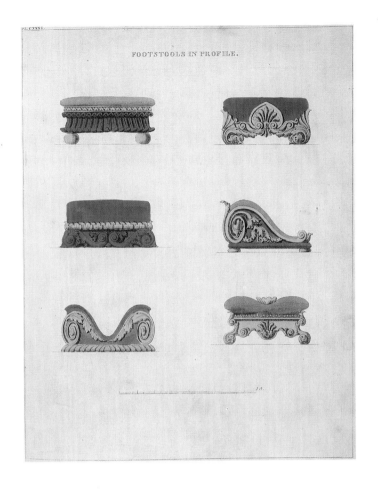

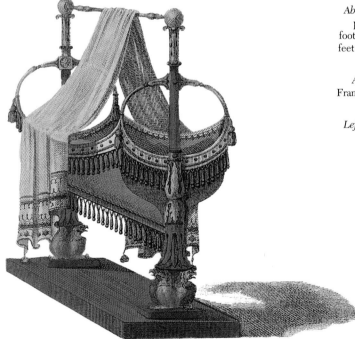

Above left: Upholstered furniture played an important part in Regency interiors. This selection of ornate footstools with fashionable curved shapes and distinctive feet appeared in George Smith's *The Cabinet Maker and Upholsterer's Guide.*

Above right: Block-printed scenic wallpapers from France were popular in the United States as well as France. This scene, *c.*1815, consisted of 25 panels.

Left and below: An elaborate cot bed and nursery chair from Ackermann's *Repository,* 1809.

pink, saffron yellow, blues and golds, Pompeian red, and a subtle turquoise that had been favoured by Percier and Fontaine and much copied in America. Powerful colours were often used with tints of their complementaries.

The French Empire colours were also strong, reflecting the optimism felt in the country at the time. Empire green, Empire ruby, azure blue, clear lemon yellow, amethyst and pearl grey were all mixed with gold and white. The quieter colours in the palette were the result of Josephine's influence.

Until the 1800s green had been produced on fabrics by printing indigo over a fast yellow – this was called quercitron. It was very prone to fading, however, so when its patent ran out around 1800, it was not renewed, and a fast solid green was soon introduced.

There was now a rather different approach to the use of colour in interiors. Carpet colours were chosen to harmonize with the walls, the curtain fabrics were usually a little paler than the walls, upholstery was coordinated with the curtain fabric, and furniture paintwork was chosen to match the background colour of the wallpaper or the colour of the walls themselves. Red was very fashionable. It appeared a great deal in dining-rooms and was considered an excellent background for paintings. Green was a popular choice for drawing-rooms and libraries and was also used for wood and ironwork, screens and blinds, though one trend was to make blinds a lighter shade of the actual curtain colour. The restful quality of blue was considered to be particularly appropriate for bedrooms. Gilding was no longer fashionable except on picture frames.

From the 1830s there was a return to lighter colours, including blues, buffs, lilacs, French greys, pink and yellow. It was fashionable to use colour accents and unusual combinations such as plum and yellow. Tinted whites appeared on ceilings but were rarely used on the walls.

American Interiors

European styles were by now crossing the Atlantic more quickly. In America, the early 19th century was an era of nationalism, prosperity and growth. The country was expanding in virtually every aspect, including population, geographical size (the United States doubled in size with the Louisiana Purchase in 1803) and the arts. The American Empire style that developed during the late Federal period was characterized, as in England and France, by Classical motifs and geometric forms. Light tones were used on walls, along with richly coloured draperies and upholstery. Block-printed wallpapers, again with Classical motifs, were popular, as was stencilling. The so-called "scenic papers" from France, which formed a floor-to-ceiling panorama around a room, were very sought after in America, even though they had not caught on in England. The earliest ones had been hand-painted, but by the early 19th century they were being block-

An early 19th century American interior furnished with furniture by Duncan Phyfe, one of the country's leading cabinet makers. The restrained swags and tails with delicate fringing act as a foil to the rich wood of the furniture.

printed. Wall panelling was now either absent or restricted to the dado (the area below the chair rail).

American Empire furniture generally featured deeper carving and more elaborate ornamentation (stencilling, graining, gilding, applied ormolu mounts) than earlier pieces had. Light woods and decorative inlays were fashionable at the beginning of the period, but by 1820 these had been supplanted by mahogany and carved and gilded ornament.

The leading American furniture maker of the time – considered by many the greatest American cabinet maker ever – was Duncan Phyfe. Working from New York, where his workshops employed over a hundred men, he produced mahogany pieces based mainly on Thomas

Sheraton's pattern books, as well as the Directoire and Empire styles. Another cabinet maker of the time, the quality of whose work was at least as high but whose output was much less, was Charles-Honoré Lannuier. Mass-production techniques were developing here as elsewhere, and one innovator in this area was Lambert Hitchcock, whose gaily painted and gilded or stencilled "Hitchcock chairs" were produced from 1825.

CURTAINS AND DRAPERY

The Napoleonic Wars had a considerable influence on both sides of the Channel. In France *"le style héroique"* was inspired by all things military, and the use of motifs and decorative ornaments was closely associated with the major personalities of the war and certain battles. French-style beds with elegant trailing canopies were much in vogue. Many people see this period as the real zenith of window treatments. The curtain treatment was the focus of design in European and American rooms and gave the incumbent an opportunity to demonstrate her sense of style. The layered look that developed – combining outer curtains, under-curtains, muslin curtains and sunblinds, suspended on poles or including a deep valance – was one of great elegance and appeal. The complex and beautiful trimmings were an integral part of the design and served an important function in balancing the whole.

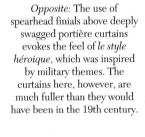

Opposite: The use of spearhead finials above deeply swagged portière curtains evokes the feel of *le style héroique,* which was inspired by military themes. The curtains here, however, are much fuller than they would have been in the 19th century.

Below: There were many interpretations of *le style héroique,* even influencing the design of bed hangings, which often had spearlike poles. As in this military couch-bed, trimmings were of the utmost importance.

Above: A French "military-style" bed, the draperies arranged in such a way as to give it a tent-like appearance. Beds such as this were often portable.

Beds and Bed Hangings

Bed drapery was beautiful but generally much simpler than in earlier periods. Typical of the period's elegance was the French Empire method of placing the bed along the wall with a centrally mounted canopy supporting curtains or draperies that trailed over the curved ends of the bed. Napoleon's bed at Fontainebleau was assembled in a military style in a rich *velours de Lyon* (velvet made in Lyons) decorated with laurel leaves and a border of roses.

The *lit bateau*, or boat-bed, so-named because of its shape, was typical of Empire beds. It often had swan's head scroll ends, the swan being a popular Empire theme, as the black swan was the Empress Josephine's emblem. Even cradles were wonderfully draped and there were some highly original treatments.

Egyptian, Gothic revival and chinoiserie styles all influenced bed treatments at this time. Drapes could still be luxurious and were usually covered and lined with contrasting or toning fabric. The rear bed curtain was often arranged in a sunburst pattern, with the ceiling of the canopy frequently executed in the same way. It was fashionable for bed linen, quilts and blankets to be white.

A domed tester bed with ornately carved and gilded cornice, swagged valance and tails hanging down at each corner over the bed curtains.

Sofa-beds were popular in the 19th century and were usually treated in the French style, being placed along the wall. Draperies that trailed over the ends of the bed were suspended from a centrally mounted canopy which was often heavily ornamented.

Far left: Carved and gilded curtain cornices, often combined with a deep valance, became a feature of the period. Here, a double border, tassel and rope detailing and undercurtains complete the treatment.

Left: For many, the early 19th century represents the golden age of window treatments. The complex but satisfyingly symmetrical build-up of drapery in patriotic colours shown here was first published in 1826.

In early 19th century America, bed valances were fuller and gathered at the base and around the tester of a four-poster bed, and the ceiling of the tester was often pleated into a central star. Sometimes the top valance was highly decorative, with scalloped edges or with different shapes sewn together to make festoons or cascades. Reefed curtains were sometimes used so that the bed curtains could be drawn up to allow air to circulate.

Windows

The conventional sash remained the most usual type of window at this time. The 19th-century version, slightly more refined than before, was often taller and narrower or arched. Glazing bars were thinner still, and the reduction of the window tax in 1815 encouraged larger windows.

The influence of homecoming English from India was felt with the appearance of verandas at first-floor level. These often extended all around the house to take advantage of the views and were combined with French windows and wood or ironwork.

Bow windows, often used in groups, were a popular feature of the period. Margin lights also became widely used in this period, with acid-etched glass in attractive patterns sometimes used in them.

Shutters were universal, usually of the folding multi-leaf type. Decorative wooden fascias were fitted to the window-head to house folding canvas sunblinds.

Curtains

The pull-up curtain proved too bulky for the taller, narrower windows of the early 19th century and so was replaced by a slimmer, draped look using pairs of curtains, which could be hung singly or double. The new window treatments were built up in layers. They were usually hung from poles which, in turn, could be suspended from a curtain cornice to give architectural impact. Rods or poles were often highly decorative, with ornaments such as laurel wreaths and rosettes. Where curtain cornices were not used, the treatment often had a draped heading above the main curtains with loops, swags or festoons. The main curtains themselves were usually floor-length or trailing on the floor. In the daytime they were caught back on cords or cloak pins to keep them out of the way. The curtains were usually lighter in colour than the walls.

Under-curtains were a great feature of the period. They were made of a lightweight fabric such as silk or muslin enlivened with delicate fringing or wide border designs, in contrasting colours such as dark green or yellow on white. The under-curtains were generally fixed to one side of the window but were occasionally drawn in order to protect the interior furnishings from strong sunlight. Definition was given with carefully placed tassels, and trimmings were heavy to ensure that the curtains hung well.

Finally, a blind of some sort would nearly always complete the treatment. These included white roller blinds, slatted blinds, chintz blinds and updated forms of sashes. It was not unusual for blinds to carry Gothic revival, chinoiserie or heraldic patterns and, in America, Classical painted scenes were particularly popular. Where the curtains were too complex to draw at night the blind was often made in a material that matched the curtains to complement the treatment when it was pulled down. The complexity and immobility of these styles was partly their undoing, as the poor hygiene of the day soon led to their becoming home to rodents and other undesirables!

External blinds were coming into fashion. They either were made of canvas or were frame-and-lath blinds with slats and were operated by a knob in the frame.

Although the window treatments looked complex, in fact they depended on simple geometric shapes for their effect, and there was a proportional system for scaling a good curtain design. All cutting was carefully considered to avoid wastage. The pinning of swags was disguised with discs or rosettes.

By the 1820s, continuous drapery had been introduced to link two or more windows on one wall and the decoration of the pole became an even more important feature. This could be moulded, painted or gilded and was almost always ornamented with motifs. As in earlier designs, these curtains were caught back on rosettes or cloakpins during the day. They were often lined in contrasting fabric. Continuous

The taste for Classical simplicity was reflected in fashion. Stiffness and formality were replaced by a softer, column-like shape. Women's gowns now had higher waists and were made in thin, plain materials. They were scanty and lightweight, and so a layered look emerged, similar in concept to the window treatments of the period.

In this Regency room, by Fine Art Interiors, fringed swags with long tails are draped over a pole. The colour of the fabric is lighter than that of the wall, lending a period feel to this dining room and complementing the Regency-style furniture. Buttoned seat cushions tied on with bows make an attractive feature.

drapery sometimes appeared in conjunction with ceiling drapery for a tented effect.

In the French Restauration period (the period following Napoleon's abdication in 1814), scarf drapery in different fabrics and contrasting colours typified the epoch. Walls were lavishly draped and curtains were thick and heavy with elaborate trimmings.

In Biedermeier interiors, window treatments were kept simple to allow in as much light as possible. A typical approach featured asymmetrically draped sheers trimmed with tassels and fringes.

In America curtains were in much more general use; they were no longer confined just to the grander homes. New styles were now used, especially in the more important rooms, and layered drapery started to replace pull-ups and paired curtains. The layered look from France and England needed skilful execution, and James Arrowsmith's

Analysis of Drapery was an important reference book of the period. When Thomas Jefferson ordered curtains for Monticello, he submitted rough sketches of his requirements to the suppliers. Formal swag-and-tail or draped pelmets in silk, with muslin under-curtains, were a standard treatment for a stylish room in the Federal period.

There was not always a high standard of finish. Few curtains were lined or interlined in America, and they were often assembled without regard to pattern matching. Pleats might be fixed with nails or tape, and many curtains were simply nailed to the actual frame. As in France and England, continuous drapery was used where there were two or more windows together on the same wall, and decorative poles and curtain cornices were also a feature. Ideas were taken from George Smith's *A Collection of Designs for Household Furniture and Interior Decoration* (1808) and Ackermann's *Repository*.

In smaller American homes, curtains were often white dimity and would sometimes have the addition of a paper border or draped shawl for a stylish effect. Now that pull-up curtains had gone out of fashion, it became much easier to apply paper borders around the room, as the pulled-up fabric had covered the gap between the ceiling cornice and window architrave.

Fabrics

The highly improved dyeing and printing techniques of the early 19th century resulted not only in more realistic colours for floral designs but also in vastly reduced prices as textiles could now be produced in bulk. This, in turn, began the decline of Britain's silk industry. Elaborate brocaded silks were no longer so fashionable, though other silks from Genoa, Lyons and London's Spitalfields were still popular, as were tulle, lustrous taffeta, velvets, damasks, satin, printed linen, sprigged muslin and printed cotton chintz.

Pattern and texture were important, and merino wool, Manchester velvets (cottons with small patterns stamped on – the name comes from the fact that Manchester was the centre of the English roller-printing industry), machine-pressed watered fabrics, geometric and architectural designs, trellis patterns, columns and stripes were all sought after. Fabrics in the Chinese taste, which had faded away at the end of the 18th century, were very much in vogue again.

Motifs on fabrics were popular, especially in France, and featured Napoleonic bees, swans, laurel wreaths, crowns, lyres, vases, the initials of the Emperor, eagles, oak leaves and the like. The production of Lyons silk was flagging at the start of the Empire period, but Napoleon's support, combined with major mechanical advances, breathed new life into the industry. When the monarchy was restored in France, Empire ornaments on fabric designs were altered, with the Fleur-de-lis replacing the Napoleonic bee and the L for Louis XVIII replacing the N for Napoleon.

Exquisite *passementerie* played a vital part in the definition and balance of curtain treatments of this period, often providing the necessary weight to keep the drapery in place. Specialist companies can now produce superb copies of the originals using wooden mouldings and tassels.

Trimmings

Trimmings were strong, rich and varied and had an important role to play, giving weight and balance to the furniture and the complex window treatments.

The trimmings for curtains grew heavier at this time. In some instances, the fringing was actually made up of wooden pendants covered in silk and decorated. There was a wide variety of fringing, much of it delicate and knotted. Braids, which were often applied to curtains, were delicate in design and used against a contrasting colour, such as a braid of white flowers against a strong green fabric.

The bronze and gilt rosettes, discs and cloakpins used to hold back the curtains became increasingly decorative in their own right.

Plain fabrics were made more interesting with the addition of contrasting linings and appliquéd or painted borders.

Trimmings were extremely expensive when made professionally and so were often imitated by ladies at home. Amateur accomplishments of this sort were very fashionable and extended to open work, handpainted velvet, stencilled borders and even wallpapers.

6

THE MID TO LATE 19TH CENTURY

The Battle of the Styles

There was a great conflict between tradition and reform in the mid to late 19th century, manifested in three fundamentally different approaches to the decorating of interiors. One approach entailed careful research and attempts to recreate a past style accurately. A second approach was less concerned about authentic detail and aimed simply to capture the spirit of an earlier style. Finally, there was eclecticism – the cheerful mixing of a number of styles. There were so many style revivals coexisting and being freely combined that the whole chaotic scene is often described as the "battle of the styles".

In the first half of the century a very simple Greek style had developed (particularly in America), as well as so-called Italian, Elizabethan, Tudor, Baronial, Louis XIV (also called "Old French") and Rococo (Louis Quinze) styles. The Gothick style of the 18th century had never completely died out, and there was a Gothic revival ("Gothick" with a "k" is generally reserved for the 18th century version) in Europe and especially, America; in France it was known as the Troubadour style and in Italy as the Dantesque style. As the century progressed, interior decoration grew increasingly heavy and ornate. In most European countries and in America at around mid-century there was a Louis Seize revival, which was superseded in the 1860s–1870s by a neo-Renaissance style (epitomized in America by Stanford White). In the second half of the century, the exotic "Moorish" style was also popular, characterized by the Moorish arch form, highly patterned walls and Turkish corners (see page 154).

It was considered perfectly acceptable to combine several of these styles in one home (even in one room). The curvilinear, lighthearted neo-Rococo might be used in the drawing-room; the richly opulent Gothic revival in the library; the neo-Elizabethan, with its strapwork effects, in the dining-room; the exotic Moorish style in the smoking-room; the heavy gilding of the Louis Seize revival in the boudoir. None of these treatments would have been authentic. Indeed, many of the styles differed only superficially. The three Louis styles in particular were often confused and intermixed.

Button-backed velvet-covered chairs, throws, cushions and clutter are typical of mid 19th century interiors. Swags and tails were one of the most popular styles of window treatment. Here, lace under-curtains are used, but blinds were a fashionable alternative.

127

The neo-Renaissance style was widely popular in the 1860s and '70s. This New York family were painted in the neo-Renaissance library of their Park Avenue mansion in 1871. The deep, flat pelmets were a feature of the period on both sides of the Atlantic and were often referred to as lambrequins.

INFLUENCES

Since the latter part of the 18th century, the Industrial Revolution had been developing, and industrialization had dramatically changed people's homes as well as their lives. Because machinery could now reproduce almost any historical architectural detail, a dull uniformity settled on interior decoration. Manufacturing was increasingly aimed at the tastes of the mass market.

In order to create something very different from what everyone else had, the rich took to acquiring entire interiors, often dismantling a complete room and re-assembling it elsewhere! There began to be a reaction against the poor design and quality resulting from mass production and an appreciation of individualized craftsmanship and the beauty of the environment. The newly prosperous middle-class businessman now looked to the architects of the day for something different from the grand country house of previous centuries. He wanted traditional building materials used in an original way.

This was the background to the design reform movements that arose in the second half of the 19th century. Already, in the 1830s, the architect A.W.N. Pugin had rejected the sham Gothic and Rococo and initiated a more authentic, purist approach. Advocating a return to medieval designs and craftsmanship, he maintained that Gothic was the only true style. He believed in "honest construction", deplored the Rococo style and loathed any form of sham. Pugin gave the Gothic revival a new morality and seriousness, not only through his ideas but through his Gothic revival churches and his designs for the decoration of London's Houses of Parliament.

Pugin's ideas considerably influenced the writer and art critic John Ruskin, and the architect and poet William Morris, leading to the formation of the Arts and Crafts Movement, of which Morris was the guiding light. They believed in the virtue of honest design, top-quality materials, craftsmanship and traditional skills, and the importance of beautiful surroundings. Maintaining that the Middle Ages was the golden age of craftsmanship, the craftsmen of the Arts and Crafts Movement formed themselves into medieval-style guilds. In fact, William Morris's use of natural forms translated into flat patterns was at once a synthesis of medievalism and modernism, and he was the 19th century's most influential designer.

Morris's ideas were influential not just in Britain but also in America, where Arts and Crafts was known as the Craftsman style. Its best-known designers were Elbert Hubbard and Gustav Stickley, who maintained that form should follow function. Stickley also edited the magazine *The Craftsman*, which promulgated the movement's ideas throughout America. Its leading exponent was the young architect Frank Lloyd Wright, who at the end of the century was designing Arts and Crafts furniture, metalwork and stained glass for his "Prairie Houses". It was Wright who introduced mechanization to American Arts and Crafts despite its being anathema to the movement's purists.

A typical English Arts and Crafts cottage would be low-ceilinged, be built of local materials, and contain an inglenook fireplace, ledge-and-brace oak doors, wide polished floorboards, oak furniture and stencilled friezes.

One of the most successful designers of the time was the architect C.F.A. Voysey. A member of the Arts and Crafts Movement, he soon developed his own lighter, more elegant style. He is regarded as one of the English designers who pioneered the style that developed into Art Nouveau (see page 132), but Voysey himself dismissed Art Nouveau as "revolting".

Voysey also had little time for the Aesthetic Movement, another reform movement that arose in the last quarter of the century in England and America (though not on the Continent). Reacting against what it described as the "philistine" taste of the Victorian era, the Aesthetic Movement believed in art for art's sake. It denied, however,

"Fool's Parsley", a design for a wallpaper by the highly influential designer C.F.A. Voysey, a member of the Arts and Crafts Movement.

that art had any social or moral value, and this set it apart from the Arts and Crafts Movement. The Aesthetic style also tended to be more exotic and sophisticated in approach; it was this movement that led to the use of white walls and ceilings to give a feeling of space. It was influenced by japonaiserie, the fashion for Japanese decoration which had followed the opening of Japanese ports to trade with the West in the middle of the century. The architect E.W. Godwin was the leading designer in the Anglo-Japanese style and one of the principal figures of the Aesthetic Movement.

In the 1860s and '70s a number of English architects, notably Richard Norman Shaw, reacted against the Gothic revival and sought inspiration in vernacular architecture (leading to what was known as the Old English style) and the late 17th century, particularly the architecture of Christopher Wren (resulting in the Queen Anne revival style). The Queen Anne style house, in red brick with a tiled roof, was a mixture of Classical features, Georgian sash windows and Dutch

Opposite: The Arts and Crafts Movement brought a new emphasis on quality and simplicity. Curtains were no longer a dominant part of the interior decoration and were pared down to the minimum.

The use of white paint, white fabric and rose motifs is very characteristic of the work of Charles Rennie Mackintosh and the Glasgow School. This is The Hill House, the most important domestic building Mackintosh designed.

gables. It was enthusiastically embraced in America where, with the addition of verandas, decorative detail and informal planning, the houses became highly individual. Queen Anne revival furniture was also produced, in England principally by E.W. Godwin and in the United States by the Herter brothers.

Another highly influential turn-of-the-century British architect designing houses in the Queen Anne style was Edwin Lutyens. Lutyens also worked in the Tudor vernacular style and neo-Renaissance style, before settling on a Classical style in the early 20th century.

Art Nouveau first appeared in the 1880s, reaching the height of its popularity in 1900. It influenced architecture and all aspects of interiors in Belgium, France, Austria, Germany, Italy and Spain, finding particular favour in Italy, where beautiful glass and ironwork were produced. In England and America, however, it really only affected wallpapers, textiles and the decorative arts. Even the work of Charles Rennie Mackintosh and the Glasgow School, with their rather severe version of Art Nouveau, had more impact on the Continent, especially on the artists of the Wiener Werkstätte, whose version of Art Nouveau was known as Sezessionstil. With its asymmetric, curvilinear designs and whiplash curves, Art Nouveau was influenced by Rococo, the Arts and Crafts Movement and japonaiserie. The earliest examples of the style are believed to be an 1883 book illustration and some textile designs by Arthur Mackmurdo, the English architect and designer who was a friend of Ruskin and Morris and who founded the Century Guild. Mackmurdo's designs are thought to have been influenced by the "bizarre silks" with their asymmetric floral patterns combined with jagged lines, which were woven in the early 18th century. In America Louis C. Tiffany created wonderfully coloured, ornate Art Nouveau interiors, featuring stained glass windows.

Eclecticism reigned supreme in America throughout the mid to late 19th century. One style that stood out at the end of the century was the Beaux-Arts, which took its name from the large number of architects living in the United States who had been trained at the École des Beaux Arts in Paris. The style encompassed a variety of historical styles, such as the French Château, the Italian Palazzo and the Elizabethan Manor House. Comfort and harmonious living were the main priorities, and these lavish homes came equipped with mechanical communication devices, sophisticated bathrooms and kitchens, elevators and electrical systems.

In France, the style that had followed the restoration of the Bourbon monarchy in 1815 and lasted till the Revolution of 1830, known as the Restauration style, was basically a heavier version of Empire style. This was succeeded by the Louis-Philippe style, or *le style Pompadour*, which was France's Rococo revival. Coexisting with these was the country's Gothic revival, known as the Troubadour style. The Second Empire style followed, during the period (1852–1870) that Napoleon III was France's new emperor. The Empress Eugénie, who identified not so much with Josephine as with Marie Antoinette, made French 18th century furnishings, particularly Louis Seize, a symbol of style and wealth. Although this Louis revival lacked the restraint of the originals, it became the accepted international style for the grander interior. France too found herself in an era devoted to diversity and imitation. The eclectic style of the Second-Empire designer Michel Liénard, who was inspired by the Renaissance and the 17th and 18th centuries, captured the essence of this.

Italy too had a Louis revival, though it did not last so long as in other European countries. In Austria and Germany, the Biedermeier style had remained to the fore, but by the 1840s in Austria and the 1860s in Germany, neo-Louis was all the rage. Just as its popularity was falling off in the 1870s, King Ludwig II of Bavaria gave it a new lease of life.

The Scandinavians followed a similar course to the French and British, with a huge variety of styles dominating the 1800s, leading to a reaction against excess decoration by the end of the century. The

This table is by Hector Guimard, who designed the Art Nouveau entrances to the Paris Métro. With its sinuous lines and use of organic motifs, it is typical of Art Nouveau.

impetus for change came from artist Carl Larsson's three delightful books of drawings and watercolours of his own house. This light, bright house became a catalyst for reform and the basis for some of the best elements in Swedish interiors.

LIFESTYLE

The new middle class was one of the most important influences on English interiors at this time. The home had become a place in which to spend leisure time and, more significantly, a symbol of status and achievement. It was really the small house or villa that typified the buildings of the period. The husband would go out to work while his wife, with some help, would manage the home, and so the home environment became the focus of her life. The appearance of a home made a statement about the family that resided there. Fashionable furniture and furnishings, polish and cleanliness showed pride in the home and evidence that staff were employed.

Social change was affecting interior decoration too. There were now fewer girls willing to go into domestic service, as factories, commerce and department stores often offered much more attractive work, and therefore there were not so many skilled needlewomen in domestic employment. This together with the obsession with health and hygiene resulted in simpler bed and window treatments.

There were definite conventions for the uses of rooms, their furniture and their colour schemes. Certain areas were for entertaining and others for privacy. In larger homes extra wings were installed with staircases for different uses, while in smaller homes the front part was usually kept for entertaining and the back for family use. Interior layouts were now changing too, with interconnecting suites to be replaced by corridors off which individual rooms were sited. Most houses had at least two reception or entertaining rooms.

Halls were very prestigious. As they gave the first impression to the visitor, status needed to be established here. A separate dining-room was considered important and was regarded mainly as a masculine preserve, as was the library. The drawing-room was used for receiving guests before and after the evening meal; it had originally been called the withdrawing-room because the women "withdrew" there, and was considered a female space. In some houses there was a parlour or second sitting-room for family use only. Bedrooms were now much more private places than they had been in the 18th century; even brothers and sisters were separated. Rooms for servants were usually in the basement or attic, quite separate from the family accommodation, and were furnished as cheaply and plainly as possible. The end of the century saw the addition of the bathroom wherever possible. Bathtubs, washbasins and even lavatories could be lavishly

Red and green were fashionable colours in the second half of the 19th century. The green walls, dress curtains and balloon-back chairs combined with the red pull-up blind and lace curtains evoke a feeling of the period in this modern room.

decorated, but it wasn't until after World War I that running water in a bathroom could be taken for granted. Built-in furniture was an innovation of the period, with window seats, niches and cupboards. The "cottage" look was much sought after, and bungalows were introduced.

There were now many books available offering decorating advice, and it became possible to produce fashionable interiors without employing a decorator. To the modern eye the decoration of the period would seem very rich and overcrowded, with a profusion of small objects. Glass was now much cheaper to produce and, as a result, large overmantel mirrors became fashionable, and overmantels themselves were developed for the display of decorative objects. Heavily patterned and textured wallpapers were hung in the main rooms, while leaf- and flower-patterned prints were a popular choice for bedrooms. Almost every available area was stencilled, gilded or decorated in some way. Walls were still often divided into separate sections (dado, infill

An example of neo-Louis Seize style. The rather heavy-handed 19th century interpretation seems to diminish the original charm, as was often the case.

A French neo-Rococo treatment from 1890, with shallow swagged valance, small tails, rosettes and tassels for definition.

161ᵉ Livᵒⁿ

L'AMEUBLEMENT
Collection simple

Tentures, Pˡ 1427

161ᵉ Livᵒⁿ

L'AMEUBLEMENT
Collection simple

Tentures, Pˡ 1428

D. Guilmard

Midart lith.

Imp. Walter Fʳᵉˢ

CROISÉE DE SALON - Louis XVI

CROISÉE DE SALON - Louis XV.

Etoffe de la maison

Passementerie de la maison

Ornements de la maison L. NOURY.

Cᵗ BOUHOURS - JUIGNÉ Sᵗ

A. DEFORGE

Publié par D. GUILMARD, Rue de Lancry, 2, Paris.

and frieze) by the skirting board (baseboard), dado rail (chair rail), picture rail and cornice, and each part given a different treatment. However, by the end of the century, it had become fashionable to remove the dado rail, and paper the area from picture rail to skirting. Washable wallpapers were introduced, and there were innovations in flooring with complex parquetry and linoleum.

The French too were showing a tendency to over-decorate their interiors. The upholsterer played an important part in this, resulting in a profusion of upholstered seats known as *pouffes* and *crapauds* (meaning "toads") and a rash of settees for two to three people with names like *confidantes à deux places* and *indiscrets à trois places* or *canapés a l'amitié* which evoked an atmosphere of pneumatic bliss!

For many countries, the Biedermeier style (see page 108) still offered the ideal solution. It was acceptable at different social levels and relied more on decoration than on an actual architectural style. By 19th century standards it was a sparse and simple style – homely and unpretentious yet elegant. Floors were usually wooden, rugs and walls were brightly painted or papered in fine stripes or small flower patterns, and the ceiling was usually white. Paintings were simply framed and hung in rows while the furniture itself was small but comfortable and serviceable. A particular feature of Biedermeier, derived from the Empire style, was to drape the walls with gathered fabric which would then be caught back in bunches to reveal mirrors.

Overstuffed French upholstery of the mid 19th century included the *crapaud* armchair and the *indiscret* (a three-seater sofa also known as a conversation seat).

Furniture and Upholstery

The mid 19th century brought balloon-back chairs and sofas and the introduction of coil-springing, usually accompanied by deep-buttoning. Upholstery was luxuriant and curvy, though by the 1880s buttoning was already out of fashion.

Velvet was the preferred fabric for upholstery, though needlepoint and Berlin wool work (a very popular new form of multicoloured needlepoint, worked from printed charts) were also used. Later in the century, loose covers were made from striped fabric or floral chintz. Dining chairs were usually covered in stamped leather or tapestry. Aesthetic chairs, and also Eastlake furniture (see page 143), were often upholstered in two different cloths.

Arts and Crafts seating included close-covered bench seats and ladder-back chairs with rush seats. The simplicity and solidity of Philip Webb's austere oak furniture epitomized Arts and Crafts furniture.

Mahogany and, later, walnut and satinwood were the most popular woods for furniture. Dark oak was used for neo-Elizabethan, Gothic revival and Arts and Crafts pieces. Papier-mâché furniture, usually lacquered black and then decorated, became popular for the first time, and bentwood furniture was developed in Germany around the middle of the century. A feature of the period was dressing tables lavishly draped in muslin or calico.

This dressing table, with its ornate canopy, the entire structure heavily draped in muslin, is typical of the period.

Leighton House, the former home of Victorian artist Lord Leighton, has recently been completely restored. The designers, Susan Llewellyn Associates, had only black-and-white pictures for reference for this room, so the wonderful yellow damask was selected with the skilled help of Britain's Victorian Society.

Colours

This was a time of magnificent, rich colouring, with interior colour schemes highly prescribed. Red was almost mandatory for dining-rooms. Libraries and studies tended to be plain and severe, with unpatterned fabrics and quiet colours. Drawing-rooms, boudoirs and bedrooms were the most opulent and colourful rooms in the house, often in strong blue. Halls and stairways were sometimes in neutral tones or in very dark shades for maximum practicality. Colours used at this time included Pompeian red, buff, taupe, tobacco and chocolate brown, Stuart and olive green, indigo and Prussian blue, burgundy, black and gold.

The 1890s were often known as the "mauve decade", due to William Perkin's discovery of the first artificial dyes in 1856, which resulted in new and brilliant purples and pinks. The colours "magenta" and "solferino", named after battles in the Austro-Italian War of 1859, were the most popular shades of the new dyes.

In France during the Louis-Philippe epoch (the two decades prior to the establishment of the Second Empire) it was fashionable to

American Gothic in a Louisiana antebellum (pre-Civil War) plantation house. The colours are much brighter and more vivid than those usually associated with the Gothic revival, and the delicately bordered sheer curtains under the Gothic revival pelmets less heavy. This wing of the house was built especially to house the vast and splendid bed.

decorate rooms entirely in one colour such as blue or green. The Second Empire style in France is associated with red, orange, blue and bright pink.

Neo-Renaissance interiors were predominantly red and brownish-black. The colours associated with Art Nouveau were pale and included mauve pinks, greens, turquoise, blue and yellow. The Arts and Crafts Movement had a subtle palette of olive green, hyacinth blue, plum, burgundy, lemon yellow, taupe, old rose, ivory, pale grey and white. In collaboration with Thomas Wardle, the most skilled British dyer of the late 19th century, William Morris revived the art of using vegetable dye. Morris and Wardle experimented with four basic colours, red, yellow, brown and blue and produced indigo, pale orange, a grey-green, brown orange and garnet red.

OVERLEAF:

The drawing room of a mid 19th century Mississippi home. The green and gold brocade curtains are hung on ornate poles under pelmets with rope and tassel trimmings.

American Interiors

By the middle of the 19th century, American styles were virtually the same as those prevailing in England. The Gothic revival style, which had taken over from the American Empire and Greek revival styles in the 1840s, was grand and stately, with lavish use of draped hangings and curtains on windows, beds, walls and ceilings. Favourite fabrics were velvets, velours and brocatelles. Lugubrious colours such as maroon, dark green and brownish-black were combined with patterned carpets, often in pale blues and reds. Pointed arches and pierced tracery were commonly used motifs on the furniture and decoration.

The Elizabethan revival which developed in the 1850s was characterized by heavy furniture inspired by 16th century English pieces. The Rococo revival, with its richly carved rosewood and walnut furniture, and the Renaissance revival, with massive, richly decorated, rectilinear pieces, also became popular at about this time. The leading furniture designers of these styles were John-Henry Belter and Léon Marcotte respectively. From the 1860s to about 1870 the neo-Louis Seize style was fashionable.

Eastlake-style furniture became commonplace at this time too. Inspired by the designs of the English architect Charles Eastlake, who also designed wallpaper, textiles, tiles, etc., it was basically simple, solid and of sound craftsmanship. Eastlake is perhaps best known for his book *Hints on Household Taste*, which had enormous impact in both England and, even more so, America, where furnishings in the "improved" taste were said to be "Eastlaked". With regard to soft furnishings, Eastlake recommended tight-fitting upholstery and heavy curtains, without applied fringe, hanging straight from rings on poles that were not overlarge. He also popularized horizontally striped curtains and portières (see page 149).

Gustav Stickley's Mission Oak furniture and Elbert Hubbard's Roycroft furniture were in a similar vein to Eastlake's: simple, honest, craftsman-made oak pieces in the Arts and Crafts mould, which were nevertheless distinctly American in style.

Drapery was taken to extremes in the latter half of the 19th century. Even the backs of pianos were covered in fabric, and chimney breasts were ornately swagged and swathed.

CURTAINS AND DRAPERY

Opposite: Resplendent purple swags and tails with outsize rosettes frame doors to the conservatory in this 19th century English painting. The room is decorated in the "Chinese taste", which had briefly come back into fashion with the Rococo revival of the middle of the century.

By mid-century a proliferation of styles existed, and curtaining was more lavish than ever. Curtains were not only used on windows, doors and beds: as time went by they found their way onto chimney breasts and pianos! So much fabric was used that the rooms seemed very dark. Heavy trimmings and blinds were essential parts of any treatment. By the end of the century there came the inevitable reaction to this claustrophobic look, and bed and window drapery became lighter and simpler along with interior decoration in general.

A typical mid 19th century window treatment. Bay windows were common in Victorian homes, and swags and tails were especially useful for disguising awkward corners. The lacy sheers caught back and cloakpins are also typical. Blinds were an indispensable part of a window treatment; they were sometimes decorative but more often plain green, like these.

Beds and Bed Hangings

As health and hygiene became major concerns in the latter part of the 19th century, heavy bed drapery began to be viewed as unhealthy, and a lighter look emerged. When F. Heal & Son was first established, they specialized in supplying portable furniture for army officers abroad. By the 1850s they were offering portable half-tester beds, portable tent bedsteads with mosquito netting and portable French beds. They also supplied the fabric for drapery and all the bedding including quilts. By 1880 the informative catalogue was showing at least 12 different ways to drape a half-tester bed.

Simplicity was the key to Arts and Crafts beds, with the emphasis on the quality of fabric design. Plain cornice boxes in wood, painted or covered with a simple stiffened pelmet, were used in conjunction with paired curtains. Sometimes the cornice boxes were omitted to show curtains on their track. Beds were mainly undraped, with wooden or brass bedsteads. Bedcovers were handmade, perhaps in lace or quilting. Four-poster beds with plain curtains and a straight valance were a popular choice.

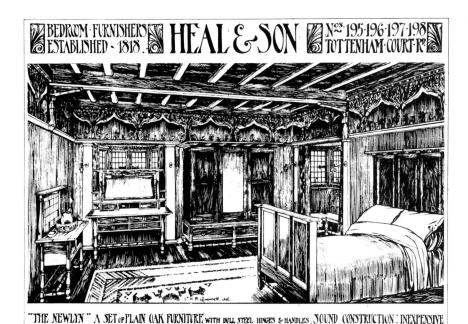

"THE NEWLYN" A SET OF PLAIN OAK FURNITURE WITH DULL STEEL HINGES & HANDLES . SOUND CONSTRUCTION : INEXPENSIVE

A simple Arts and Crafts style bed in Heal's 1893 catalogue. The design for the bedroom included an oak ceiling and decorative plaster frieze.

Windows

In 1851 the window tax was finally abolished, and this, combined with vastly improved glass-making techniques which produced stronger, cheaper panes of glass needing fewer glazing bars, resulted in wider windows. Typical of the period were bay windows with a wide centre sash and two narrower lights at either side. The sash window was still in use, but was plainer and surrounded by increasingly decorative brickwork. In the late 1800s some sashes had smaller panes of glass and thicker glazing bars to reduce glare. Gothic and Tudor-style windows were popular, especially in smaller houses. Arch-topped windows with decorative tracery to reduce sunlight and protect interior furnishings from fading were evident in some of the grander houses. One innovation was the pivoting sash window for easy cleaning.

A typical Art Nouveau window would have had no decorative surround and would have been set flush with the wall. Stained glass was very much a part of this style and appeared on sashes, casements and even French windows. Many designs were elaborate, depicting birds or plants, while sometimes they were in abstract shapes. Stained glass was often used on staircase or landing windows for privacy.

The Arts and Crafts Movement experimented with a number of different window shapes, but the Queen Anne style sash was preferred. As light and air were considered important with this style, bay, oriel and rows of dormer windows were in vogue.

Designs combining windows and glazed doors were fashionable, as were window seats and leaded lights.

In the latter half of the century new methods of production enabled steel-framed windows to compete with those made from wood. Casement windows were mass-produced and the frames inserted straight into the prepared brick or stone openings. In very expensive houses, windows made of gunmetal or bronze were favoured, as these windows did not require painting and were therefore considered maintenance-free.

Bay windows remained a characteristic of the terraced house. Cottage-style windows were also much in evidence. A favourite colour combination for painting windows was green and cream.

Curtains

Curtains did not escape the proliferation of styles and revivals in Victorian interiors. It was not uncommon to find, say, a "Gothic revival" portière with a "neo-Rococo" lambrequin. The upholsterer became a general supplier for curtains and loose covers and could also supply craftsmen to decorate interiors, which resulted in a much more coordinated look. Curtains were generally hung from poles, and swags and tails were used a great deal. This was especially the case in drawing-rooms, where the curtains were often "dress" curtains (designed not to pull across the window) tied back on rosette-headed pins with sheers underneath. Decorative finials on the poles were an important part of the treatment. Everything was fringed, braided and bobbled.

As the century progressed, the same sort of excesses that existed in interiors could be found in the costume of the day, which was covered with applied trimmings such as tucks, flounces, frills, ruching, piping, binding and artifical flowers.

Sometimes the light was kept out altogether by the use of blinds. These were usually made of Holland linen (a type of canvas) though brown Holland was sometimes considered too dark. Blinds could also be painted, bordered or self-patterned and trimmed with fringes or borders. Some of the painting executed on the blinds was very beautiful and detailed, and landscapes were popular. A cheap version of the roller blind was wallpaper pasted onto linen.

The lambrequin made a reappearance in the Victorian era. Confusingly, the French referred to their 17th century flat pelmets as lambrequins (see page 41), but the Victorian version was a flat pelmet with a shaped outline which continued down the side of the window, sometimes as far as the floor. Designs for these were first seen in America in *The Workwoman's Guide* (1838). Originally the lambrequin was intended to hide the bunches of fabric formed when a pull-up curtain was drawn above the window but it soon became a treatment in its own right. It could be combined with symmetrical main curtains

below and often also had an asymmetrical muslin one, caught back in different tie-backs. Lambrequin shapes varied with fashion but the construction of stiffened buckram, paper or wood, lined with plain brown chintz or Holland, remained much the same. Sometimes they were covered with velvet or moreen and the lower edge cut into an appropriate shape. They were fixed to the window frame with nails, and any curtain rods or workings would be hidden behind them. By the end of the century, however, they were out of fashion, as they cut out too much light.

Although carefully pleated curtain headings were still not common by the end of the century, it became fashionable for valances to have

Lace incorporating delicate floral designs was a popular choice for blinds, but a variety of other fabrics and trimmings were also used, often with the addition of hand-painted designs.

147

vertical pleats extending the depth of the valance or pelmet, and these were used as an alternative to swags and tails. Those known as goblet pleats were cup-shaped and padded, making a particularly attractive heading. To add interest, pelmet boards were built out in either a semi-circular or a rectangular shape and covered with a pleated pelmet.

Draped pelmets or valances were used where a flat lambrequin or pelmet would have seemed too severe or stiff. They could be draped over or around the pelmet or be used as an ornament on the pelmet itself, so they needed to be of a lightweight fabric that would drape well in small units.

Swags and tails were a satisfactory treatment for the many bay windows of the period as they covered the awkward corners. The draperies were, of course, cut and put together to give the impression of one piece of fabric.

At this time scarf drapery, where one piece of fabric was skilfully draped to make a heading for a treatment, became fashionable. It was also used to decorate shop windows and for bunting and exhibition stands. The Art Nouveau influence was apparent in the elaborate, asymmetrically arranged festoons.

Pelmets were seen in a variety of period styles, including Grecian, Gothic, Elizabethan, Moorish and Louis XIV, and were sometimes hung behind the actual curtains. By mid-century, stamped brass or richly gilded pelmet cornices were often placed on top of the fabric pelmets. Around the end of the century a Louis-style drawing-room was the ultimate look – curvaceous, glamorous and obviously expensive.

Muslin curtains were still used to exclude insects and soften the light. White curtains were generally in vogue, especially in America, where they were often swagged back over a curtain rosette or cloakpin and fastened to the window frame. White cotton dimity was used extensively for bed curtains and counterpanes.

Portières were popularized by many designers, especially Charles Eastlake, at this time. They were often double-sided, so that each fabric would harmonize with the colour scheme of the room it faced. Appliqué or embroidery was frequently added to divide them into horizontal bands corresponding to the frieze, infill and dado of the adjacent walls.

In 1855 F. Heal & Son opened a curtain department. They sold damasks, velvets, plushes, reps and printed or striped fabrics for curtains and upholstery. Venetian, spring roller and festoon blinds were all offered in their catalogue, and their window poles were of wood or brass. In 1893 they began to show room sets in their Tottenham Court Road store displaying examples of Parisian drapery. Harrods' catalogue carried a similar list.

One of the biggest influences on window treatments in America towards the end of the century was Frank Moreland's book, *Practical*

A modern version of the scarf drapery that was fashionable in the 19th century. The deep swag and long, delicate fringe provide added interest.

Decorative Upholstery, which first appeared in 1889. Moreland had worked for about 40 years for Shepard, Norwell & Co., who had one of the most comprehensive drapery and upholstery departments in America at that time. Not only did he give clear instructions on how to execute fashionable drapery and upholstery but he also held very definite views on soft furnishing which he passed on to his readers.

For drawing-rooms he recommended long curtains with pelmets or curtains carried into festoons (swags) at the top and always lace curtains underneath. Where there was more than one window on a wall, he advised long curtains, one at each end of the room, with the windows linked together by a pelmet or valance in order to provide a decorative treatment that gave maximum light. The feeling of continuity was to be increased by using the same trim on curtains and pelmet.

Dining-rooms were to be more restrained; he recommended plain curtains in plush or plain velour with the addition of appliqué or embroidery. One unusual suggestion was the use of grillwork instead of a pelmet or pelmet board. He advocated subtle colours such as gold, olive green or orange-red to contrast with ebonized woodwork, or stronger colours to contrast with natural-coloured woods such as oak or ash.

At this time in the United States, light French-style furnishings were in fashion, and woodwork in white or old ivory was picked out with gold, while walls and ceilings were usually in delicate tints. Popular fabrics were tapestry with floral designs in natural colours, and silk or brocatelles in subdued colours.

Moreland recommended portières (silk plush with painted flowers was one suggestion for a boudoir), lace curtains, glass curtains (short curtains inside the window casing, usually for privacy), in silk muslin or madras trimmed with fringing, cottage curtains with shirred tops, festoon blinds, Austrian curtains and special-purpose drapery for mantelpieces (which he designed as "tasteful drapery of scarfs of silk in dark colours to show mantel ornaments") and dressing tables. Plain or figured silks, cretonnes, chintz, printed sateens, cream and ecru madras trimmed with coloured ribbons, or muslin with box-pleated silk ribbon or soft ball fringe were all suggested for dressing tables. Moreland was of the opinion that the bedchamber should be quiet, restful and harmonious, and he preferred the half-tester to be presented as a continuation of the room cornice. He advised that bedhangings should be sympathetic to window curtains though not necessarily *en suite*.

Moreland's book covers six different types of curtain, all of which were obviously fashionable at the time: festoon blinds; French drapery, where separate pieces of fabric are put together to give the appearance of one long piece of fabric swagged over a pole; irregular drapery, where the swags were spread more to one side than the other and

A decorative lambrequin completely frames a pair of windows, with under-curtains caught back to the sides, and blinds beneath the curtains, in this late 19th century French treatment.

Shaped pelmets with Art Nouveau motifs that tie into the dado decoration add interest to these simple paired curtains from France, c. 1880. Brass holdbacks and blinds with wide borders complete the treatment.

appeared to be a continuation of the curtain; raised drapery, for treating a wide space like the central section of a bay or uniting several windows under one drapery; flat valance, combined with festoons (or swags), which used less fabric than full swags and which was often lined with buckram to preserve the flat surface; looped-up drapery, for halls or archways where the curtain was made to appear as though it were drawn up with a rope. This worked best with light materials which required no lining. More elaborate versions were used over lace curtains.

In mid to late 19th century France, there were so many different styles of curtain that it was impossible to establish a characteristic one. Fabrics were draped over everything just as they were earlier in the century. Pelmets were shaped or deeply swagged. There were romantic curtains in tulle, muslin or dentelle (lace) frilled, beribboned or "empearled". By the time of the Second Empire, decoration and comfort were working well together. Goblet pleats were used a great deal for the pelmets or portières and stair curtains. There were curtains with heavy lambrequins inspired by the Louis XIV styles, and there were liberal interpretations of other earlier styles which resulted in an elegant, charming but traditional look. By the end of the century fantasy decoration had set in in France. There was a general weakness of composition, with little grace or elegance. To a certain extent the taste of the upholsterers can be blamed for this decline in standards.

These heavily trimmed curtains and the deep, ornamented pelmet were inspired by the Louis XIV style. So often, 19th century interpretations lost the elegance and refinement of the originals.

Fabrics

Mass production was now the order of the day. From 1842, the British Copyright Act extended to three years, so in Britain the search for new designs became less frenetic. The improvements in printing and dyeing over the last 60 or 70 years had led to increased production, however, particularly of cotton goods. The idea of offering patterns in several different colourways had first appeared around 1820 and had become quite usual. There was a vast range of brilliantly coloured all-over printed cottons and, with the removal of taxation on prints in 1831, one- and two-colour unglazed cottons became relatively cheap in Britain.

During the 1840s there was a revival of interest in mid and late 18th century designs and, although at this time there was a colour-fast green available, it was considered more authentic to simulate the faded blue/green of quercitron. Victorian fabrics often had brown or black grounds and incorporated deep, rich colours in the design such as maroon, bottle-green or Prussian blue. From the middle of the century a number of new dyes were available for yellow, purple and blue-greens.

The specialist textile industry in Marseilles, which was badly affected by the number of cheaper cottons available, declined rapidly through the century, though small operations still remained. America

A pair of rich tartan, goblet-pleated curtains, combined with a fabric-covered table, give this room a Victorian feel.

continued to import fabrics from Europe but did set up some production centres of its own, some of which were founded by English emigré printers. Individual entrepreneurs grew mulberry trees and wove silk, but it was the Shaker community who were particularly successful in producing good-quality silk, mainly from Kentucky.

In Britain, Jacquard looms produced an increasing amount of small-patterned wool damasks and moreen, a worsted cloth with a wool finish which was fairly affordable. Roller-printing grew in importance, and soon dominated the textile industry, which used chemical dyes and a palette of colours inspired by Persian textiles.

Floral prints on cottons or cretonnes were popular in Victorian bedrooms, tartan and also paisley patterns were widely used and lace (mostly from Nottingham) was everywhere! Chintz remained fashionable for some time, though its popularity waned towards the end of the century under the influence of the reform movements. William Morris was very interested in textile design and favoured handblocked printing. Influenced not only by medieval art but also by Islamic, Persian and Italian Renaissance textiles, Morris believed that motifs from nature could be flattened and stylized, but that they should still look as though they were growing naturally.

There was renewed interest in chinoiserie designs of peacocks and dragons, phoenixes and flowers, and Arthur Silver of the Silver Studio favoured Oriental motifs like poppies, chrysanthemums and fruit trees in blossom. These fabrics were used to accompany the rich lacquerwork fashionable at the time.

The 1890s saw a vogue for all things Japanese inspired by the reopening of Japanese ports to trade with the West and by their input at recent exhibitions. Arthur Liberty, who founded his London store in 1875, promoted the Japanese style with blue-and-white porcelain, peacock feathers, etc., and these in turn influenced fabrics. For example, the stylized textile designs of E.W. Godwin incorporating fans and roundels were taken from Japanese blue-and-white porcelain.

The Near East also was a major influence. Turn-of-the-century houses, especially Queen Anne revival homes, often had "Turkish corners" furnished with Near Eastern textiles such as "Ottoman" velvets (featuring patterns based on ogees and pomegranates), prayer rugs and Turkish rugs, covering cushions, window seats and divans and used for draperies and portières.

Textiles for the Gothic revival in America came in rather gloomy colours and patterns of stylized stonework, ironwork or church windows. A colour scheme of red, blue and buff on a dark brown background was typical of the look.

In France, tulle muslin and dentelle were used for romantic-style curtains and bed draperies. Silk and damask decorated with flowers and exotic foliage were popular; the large flower designs dictated the way the fabrics were used. "Timbuctoo" was a tough, serviceable, new

Bearing a large flower design on chenille, this exquisite French fabric dates from c.1860.

French fabric which had a heavy rib and was striped horizontally in white, scarlet, black and yellow on a green, red or blue ground.

Trimmings

Trimmings were rich and ornate. Braid tended to be large and stylized with diverse decorative motifs. Gimp braid with clusters of bobble fringe was fashionable, and by the end of the century strong multi-coloured gimp and picot braids were curved, interlaced and increasingly delicate.

Fringes were usually deep and topped with braids bearing geometric patterns or appliquéd flowers. There were ornate bullion or ball fringes. Persian fringe had a wide border supporting "teardrops" or gradated balls; there was often an inset braid with a "Persian" design.

Tassel tops were arrow-head in shape or domed, with long and sometimes onion-shaped skirts. Some tassels were rather severe and stylized, and they were often appliquéd with golden leaves or shells.

Contrasting linings, corded edges, dark silk fringing, embroidered panels and *trompe l'oeil* valances were all features of the period, and bell pulls with braided edges, appliquéd centres and tassels were much in vogue.

7

THE EARLY 20TH CENTURY

Art Deco and Modernism

By the end of the 19th century, the reaction against overcrowded rooms was gathering strength, and interiors of the early 1900s were characterized by a new lightness and lack of clutter. During the first two decades of this century, wealthy homes were furnished in a "historic-house" style such as "baronial", neo-Renaissance, Louis Seize or Adam revival, while middle-class homes were often mock-Tudor or Jacobean revival. Nevertheless, the best-known styles of the early 20th century were Art Deco and Modernism. In their purist forms, these styles tended to be found only in the homes of the avant-garde, yet the influence of both of these uncompromisingly modern styles was widespread in Europe and America.

Art Deco was a deliberately outrageous style fashionable in the inter-war period. It took its name from the first decorative-arts exhibition following World War I, L'Exposition Internationale des Arts Décoratifs et Industriels Modernes, held in Paris in 1925. It had its origins earlier in the century, however, and by the time of the exhibition, it had already become passé among the leading designers and the avant-garde. The style was characterized by bold, flat, geometric shapes, flashes of sharp colour against a light-coloured background, and recurring stylized motifs such as the stepped ziggurat, chevron, fan and sunrays.

Modernism – or the International style as it is also called – displaced Art Deco in the late 1920s–'30s. This style had emerged from the Bauhaus, an influential German design school founded in 1919 by Walter Gropius. The Bauhaus advocated functionalism, which entailed a minimum of colour, ornament or architectural features. Following the school's closure by the Nazis in 1933, Bauhaus disciples settled in Britain and, particularly, the United States, where they influenced many designers and architects. (Appropriately enough, their philosophy, that "form follows function", had originally been formulated by the American architect Louis Sullivan, who at the turn of the century designed the first skyscrapers and who has been called the "Father of Modernism".)

A striking example of a Modernist home, *c.*1929. Curved windows were often a feature of this style, and curtains generally had simple pleated headings.

157

German and Viennese design and decoration were a great influence in Europe early this century. In this 1929 design from Munich, the green pelmet and contrasting white curtains, elegantly caught back in the Classical manner, complement the lines of the furniture.

INFLUENCES

Despite the marked unrest in Europe and the untimely death in 1910 of Britain's king, Edward VII, who had played a prominent role as peacemaker, there was no real inkling of the disasters to come at the start of what seemed a progressive and exciting new century. At the top end of European society the lifestyle remained almost unaltered, though there were some improvements in home comforts such as lighting and plumbing.

In England, tall, narrow town houses, mainly in the Neoclassical style, were built in squares and terraces to save space. The interior layout was virtually unchanged since the Victorian era. The suburbs were growing and blocks of flats were springing up in England, having already become firmly established in Scotland, continental Europe and America in the previous century. Housing for the poor was improved. Most well-to-do families had a town house and a country house; the country house was the main home. Change came more slowly for them, and fashion was of less importance.

World War I was a catalyst for dramatic change. There were virtually no servants, women did war work, grand homes were used as hospitals and ostentatious architecture and decoration seemed thoroughly inappropriate. After the war America was seen as the place of the future, with great scope for architects and designers.

As building had become very expensive in post-war Britain, there was a trend towards simpler homes and a move away from richness to naturalness and simplicity. Although the previous two decades were dominated by historical style revivals, there were now conscious efforts to break away from them. The expectations of the middle class were for something more modest, practical and economical to run. Families were reducing in size, and the trend was for smaller homes and fewer servants. Large houses were often turned into flats, and bungalows were a popular option. Built-in furniture saved space in these smaller homes, and a quieter, more homely style was in vogue.

There were a number of different influences at play during the early part of the century. Around 1904 there was a reaction against the Art Nouveau style, particularly in France. French designer André Groult, who was at the forefront of this and favoured traditional techniques enlivened with fantasy, revitalized the Restauration and Louis-Philippe styles of decoration in France, and became one of the first designers in the Art Deco style. Charles Martin was famous for his murals, which were often found in Groult's interiors and were worked mainly in grey, blue and pink.

The Oriental influence in Europe in the 18th and 19th centuries had come mainly from China but in the late 19th and early 20th centuries Japan was very influential too, particularly through the Oriental departments of stores such as Liberty's and Whiteley's in London. The Japanese had always had a great awareness of space and an innate flair for decoration. The simplicity and elegant restraint of their homes were much admired in the West after a century of rich and cluttered interiors. The lightweight structure of Japanese homes and the sparsity of furniture were of course dictated by their climate and, in particular, their frequent earthquakes. But it was the flexibility of their room arrangements, the diffusion of light and the use of decorative screens and colourful and decorative textiles that appealed to Western taste.

There was now a much more pronounced gap between the architectural design of a building and its interior decoration. Interior decorators were an innovation of the 20th century, and home decoration was a popular pastime even though the paints, wallpapers and pastes available were fairly basic.

Throughout Europe and America there was a desire to experiment and to find new styles and designs to adjust to the social realities of the day. Vienna was a centre of much innovation. There, the Wiener Werkstätte, founded in 1903 by the brilliant designer Josef Hoffman, produced handmade furniture, textiles and other decorative items that

Hepplewhite was another designer whose work was subject to fashionable interpretations at the beginning of the 20th century. This sketched design for a bedroom of the period, taken from Heal's catalogue, shows the Hepplewhite influence combined with the Edwardian preference for the "cottage style".

Like this bedroom design from 1927, Modernist interiors were noted for their light, neutral colours, streamlined fitted furniture and absence of fussy ornament. The plain, straight-hanging curtains here are enlivened with a bold modern design.

were highly influential in the West. The workshop closed in 1932. At the Bauhaus in Germany the students were taught that innovation and invention were of paramount importance. They worked on the basis of search and experimentation to find the right design solution, something that today's students accept as commonplace. Mies van der Rohe, who succeeded Gropius as director of the Bauhaus in 1930, was the greatest exponent of Modernism. His brilliant work was based on perfect proportions and the use of exciting materials such as glass, marble and chrome.

France was also a source of avant-garde ideas at the time. Le Corbusier adhered to similar ideas to the Bauhaus, maintaining that the house is a machine. The revolutionary buildings he designed maximized the light and were masterpieces of planning, while his furniture designs were along similar lines to those of the Bauhaus, rejecting the decorative in favour of the functional. Eileen Gray, who was English but had settled in Paris, was an influential designer of furniture and interiors designing in a style similar to that of Le Corbusier. Jean-Michel Frank decorated interiors in Paris and also California for the smart set; sparse and usually in natural tones, with surrealist touches (such as a sofa based on Mae West's lips, after a painting by Salvador Dali), they showed Japanese, Art Deco and Modernist influence. Paul Poiret was a fashion designer turned interior designer whose brightly coloured work was strongly influenced by Persian ornament and the colours of Diaghilev's Ballets Russes. (This touring troupe's dazzling production of *Scheherazade*, with its brilliant sets and costumes, had made an enormous impression on Paris and London in 1910–1911.)

In England the architect and designer C.F.A. Voysey's deceptively simple architecture, furniture, wallpapers and textiles formed a blueprint for a large part of Britain's suburbia as we know it today. Serge Chermayeff together with Erich Mendelsohn produced sophisticated Modernist interiors with fitted furniture, recessed lighting and an interesting use of wood veneers. The American

Another Modernist interior, Shrubs Wood in Berkshire. Built in 1934, it was the result of a collaboration between the leading Modernist architect, German-born Eric Mendelsohn, and the Russian designer Serge Chermayeff (both of whom worked in England in the '30s then subsequently moved to America). Shrubs Wood has recently been restored by its owner, designer Michael Aukett.

designer, Edward Knoblock, was instrumental in the development of a Regency revival in England in the 1920s.

In America, Frank Lloyd Wright created highly original but unpretentious architecture and designed the interiors down to the fitted and freestanding furniture. He broke up traditional spaces with low-level bookcases, expanding the feeling of space by allowing one to see into the room beyond. Donald Deskey was a leading American furniture designer of the time. His interiors and furnishings for New York's Radio City Music Hall are excellent examples of his Art Deco work. He also designed in the Moderne style, an American style of the 1920s and '30s which was similar to Art Deco but used contemporary machine-styled furnishings and which was influenced by the Austrian Wiener Werkstätte.

The Scandinavians rejected the extremes of the International style and achieved a modern look without abandoning traditional crafts. There, designers and craft organizations worked together to create a fresh approach to design in the 1920s and '30s. Finland's leading architect and designer, Alvar Aalto, was famous for his bent-plywood furniture. In Denmark the Academy of Fine Arts in Copenhagen aimed for comfort with dignity and simplicity.

In the most easily identifiable style of the early 20th century, Art Deco, exciting effects were achieved by using contrasting materials such as woods, chrome, glass, leather and lacquer. Here there was evidence of a number of different influences, including the Neoclassical style (seen in the fluted columns and use of Classical themes), Oriental design, Diaghilev's Ballets Russes and primitive art.

The philosophy of functionalism at the heart of Modernism made itself felt in the fashions of the '20s and '30s too, as ladies' clothing became long, lean and easy to wear, with much less ornamentation.

Opposite above: In England, an Adam revival, which had begun in the late 19th century, lasted until World War I, and reproduction furniture, some of it of a very high standard, was produced to cater for a growing market. This painting of an Adam revival room-set is from Harrods' 1910 catalogue.

LIFESTYLE

1900–1910 was a fashion-conscious decade in England. There were many books on interior decoration as well as the influential *Studio Magazine*, which recommended lighter colours, less clutter and more floor space. Some heavy Victorian drapery remained, with portières, complex window drapes and cloths to cover pianos, tables and fireplaces, but generally the look was becoming lighter. It was still fashionable to divide walls into several sections (although the dado rail had more or less disappeared, except in the hall) and to give each area a different design treatment. Matching suites of bedroom furniture were introduced. Most houses were lit with gas or oil but electricity was being used increasingly. Early forms of central heating emerged fuelled with coal or wood. Post-war houses usually included a bathroom, quite often situated next to the kitchen for ease of plumbing.

Servants were increasingly hard to come by, and housework was far from easy. There were no easy-care fabrics at this time – the wash

Opposite below: Another room-set from the 1910 Harrods catalogue. The neo-Rococo (Louis Quinze) style, which had developed in the mid 19th century, remained popular on both sides of the Atlantic until World War I.

An early example of John Fowler's work, this is the top floor of John Fowler's London house in about 1938, the year he joined Lady Colefax in partnership. Narrow lambrequins frame blinds which appear to be slatted but are in fact a chintz Fowler adapted from a Victorian Venetian blind document. The curtains are simple and straight-hung. The room is in the country style with which John Fowler felt most at ease.

generally was boiled up in a great round tank in the basement and wrung out by hand or mangle before being painstakingly ironed with a flat iron.

A new passion, which appeared at the turn of the century, was antique-hunting, and in 1918 the British Antique Dealers Association was founded to protect customers' interests. Department stores took full advantage of the Adam revival of the early part of the century, with special departments devoted to Adam-style furniture and furnishings. At the forefront of the Adam style was the London store Heal's, where these pieces were sold alongside well-crafted cottage-style furniture.

The 1920s brought a new distribution of wealth. Larger houses were divided into flats, and women became more independent. Some, with natural flair, set themselves up as interior decorators on a fee-paying basis and did very well helping *nouveau riche* clients who lacked the appropriate heirlooms and know-how for their new station in life. It was quite acceptable in society at this time to consult experts on clothes and interiors and it was very important to be fashionable.

The American Elsie de Wolfe was probably the first lady-decorator. An actress by profession, she was a keen amateur decorator at home and for friends. Her first professional commissions were in New York, where she created an uncluttered look against a fresh background of white or grey, with comfortable chairs covered in loose or tight chintz covers. She introduced smart Americans to French taste, and her interiors had witty touches such as painted French furniture, leopard-skin upholstery and trellis for a garden room.

The emphasis in interior design was on the use of light and space and the simplicity of form. In England, Syrie Maugham, wife of author Somerset Maugham, was at the forefront of the chill chic of the 1930s. Her opinion that "elimination is one of the secrets of interior decoration" was reflected in her famous all-white rooms with stripped reproduction French furniture, white flowers and mirrored screens. Vanessa Bell and her colleagues at the Omega workshops claimed that they could furnish an entire modern room for what Victorians would have spent on curtains and carpets alone. Mann and Fleming (Mrs. Harrington Mann and Robert Fleming) were known for stylish combinations of modern pieces and antiques. Lenygon & Morant were very grand, and Thornton Smith, Keeble & Co. and White Allom were all well-respected companies. Mrs. Guy Bethell's work was elegant, understated and timeless. In the late 1930s the interiors of Lady Colefax mixed spotted and striped fabrics, French provincial furniture, painted furniture with cracklure, and glazed chintzes for cushions and curtains. In 1938 she was joined in partnership by John Fowler.

Style-conscious homes of the '20s often had exotic Eastern influences or the distinctive look of Art Deco. Some of these designs were inspired by Greek or Egyptian forms and colours. (The Egyptian influence followed the opening of Tutankhamun's tomb in 1922.) Surface decoration was one of the main elements of the style, and wood, metal, motifs and decorative objects were also important. Walls were usually pale, in different shades of beige or off-white. Woods were light-coloured, and wallpaper borders were frequently used for definition. The fabrics were often in geometric prints or with period motifs in muted pastel tones, beiges and browns, bright oranges and mauves or lime green. Bedspreads could be in silver satin, with carpets and walls to match, and contrasting curtains. Lighting was dramatic and animal skins were a popular accessory.

Some of the houses resulting from the building boom of the late 1920s were Modernist and were characterized by flat-surfaced interiors with mouldings, fireplaces and other architectural features removed, roughcast walls in white or cream, and natural-wood floors.

Furniture was generally glass, chrome or tubular steel and there was a minimum of ornament. Although very few interiors were actually commissioned in the fully fledged and very austere Modernist style, fashionable homes did feature some of the less extreme elements, such as restrained, low-key colour schemes and much use of mirrors and glass.

John Gloag's books *Simple Furniture Arrangement* and *Simple Schemes for Decoration* were very influential. As a result of Basil Ionides's *Colour in Interior Decoration*, black and silver became a fashionable combination. There was generally a great receptiveness to changes of style, which department stores exploited to the full. The three-piece suite in patterned material became fashionable as did the display cabinet for prized possessions; the cocktail cabinet replaced the sideboard. There was considerable influence from America, with bathrooms becoming sleek, modern and marbled.

A Hollywood-style bedroom designed by Hayes Marshall of Fortnum & Mason. The unusual pelmet is made of synthetic chamois bordered with white percale. The curtain fabric carries a bird design on a beige ground.

In the 1930s came the great slump but, despite the depression, interior decorators prospered. The look was more subtle than in the '20s. Plain walls in soft beiges, eau de nil green, silver grey, pale peach, ash pink, powder blue, coral or turquoise were combined with curtain fabrics in a slightly deeper colour – chocolate or tan, deep blues and greens – for emphasis.

There was less pattern in general, though geometrically patterned rugs and textiles by the designer Marion Dorn were particularly fashionable. Abstract paintings were important accessories, light and dark woods were much in use and murals were very popular. Mirror

glass was used to give an illusion of space. The approach was more flexible, and it had become acceptable to mix styles and periods.

Bedrooms were often excessively feminine, with dressing tables swathed in fabric, bedspreads quilted and headboards buttoned. The whole look was influenced by the great Hollywood films. An American decoration book of the period advised that bedrooms should "reflect restfulness, simplicity and repose". Dining-rooms should be "cozily, even joyously furnished". More licence was apparently permissible in living rooms as "there will be assembled those with various interests and purposes". It also stated that "there seems to be a mistaken idea that the hall and drawing-room should be furnished as an advertisement of the financial standing of the owner". Some things, it seems, never change.

An unusual 1927 bed treatment from Germany. The free-standing swagged canopy decorated with metal pineapples surmounts a very plain double bed.

167

Furniture and Upholstery

There were no radical changes in upholstery in the first part of the century. The look was very traditional, with the three-piece suite dominant. In the '30s and '40s occasional chairs took on a pleasing rounded shape. Fortnum's catalogue illustrated a tubby-looking fireside chair, smartly striped in red and white satin, with "no arms to nudge your knitting" and described as "cheery and chunky as a peppermint humbug"!

The growing taste for antique furniture led to the furniture trade producing "reproduction" furniture from the beginning of the century in France, England and America.

Art Deco furniture was based on geometric shapes, with rounded corners. Pale woods, chrome, glass and ivory were combined with off-white fabric, leather, animal skins, even sharkskins. Modernist interiors made much use of streamlined built-in furniture with no ornament, and painted white. The tubular-steel chair by the Hungarian-born American architect Marcel Breuer, who had trained at the Bauhaus, revolutionized furniture everywhere, and Mies van der Rohe's steel and leather "Barcelona" chair was another modern design classic. Shaped plywood too was being increasingly used.

The Barcelona chair, 1929, was the Modernist architect and designer Mies van der Rohe's most famous piece of furniture. The buttoned black leather cushions are supported by curvaceous chromium-plated steel strips. Functional yet luxurious, it is still in production today.

Colours

In Edwardian interiors the walls were often painted in pastel tones, but details and ornaments were picked out in very bright colours, or black woodwork would be decorated with lines of silver paint. The new high-gloss enamel paints were used for both walls and woodwork. Adam-revival interiors were similarly dominated by creams and pastels, which is what Adam was believed to have used. (In fact, his colours were considerably stronger – see page 82.)

A typical early 20th century, Jacobean revival dining-room colour scheme would have been oak brown paint; curtains in plain red linen, plush or velvet; a red and brown carpet; tan cartridge paper combined with a tan-and-brown frieze featuring red poppies; and displays of blue-and-white plates. The drawing-room might have had sapphire-blue wallpaper, a frieze of copper and leather paper, blue shelves displaying blue-and-white china, a Persian carpet and rose damask curtains. Bedrooms tended to be lighter, with lemon-yellow or light blue walls.

At the beginning of the century, a particular range of pearly, unconventional colours was inspired by the glass light fittings of the American designer Louis C. Tiffany and included lavender, pink, red, turquoise, chartreuse, olive greens and soft browns. In the early '20s colours were subdued, with eau de nil, sage, cream, fawn, stone and buff being typical. In 1922 the dress designer Coco Chanel made an enormous impact at her show with a range of outfits in varying tones of beige, with flesh-coloured stockings.

This delightful German design for a monochrome dining room, dated 1927, features plain blue curtains with centrally placed tassels, against boldly patterned blue walls and striped upholstery fabric on the chairs.

The 1920s Harrods catalogue proclaimed colour to be "the new and exciting fashion in Furniture, Pottery, Curtains and Carpets". They added, "We have abolished Victorian wallpapers, cretonnes and window curtains and taken to light backgrounds and gay colours so far as carpets, cushions and hangings are concerned." Harrods at that time offered two types of furniture finish: borders and sprigs of colour painted by hand on a plain-coloured ground; and colour-combing, an adaptation of the old and artistic process of graining which produces a mass of broken colour. The catalogue described the effect: "The interplay of sapphire blue and rose, viridian green and blue, or gold and apple green, gives a piece of furniture a vibrant depth and richness. In mouldings or handles, pure colour is introduced as a sharp foil to the background."

The brilliant, often strident colour schemes of Art Deco, as in this design for fabric, owed much to Léon Bakst's dazzling costumes and sets for the Ballets Russes.

An exciting range of colours was associated with the Art Deco style in the 1920s. The neutral-coloured walls were influenced by the Bauhaus, which advocated a minimum of colour. A particular orange, deep blue and black, and red and gold, were all inspired by the Ballets Russes, following the astonishing impact of Diaghilev's 1910/11 production of *Scheherazade*, with Léon Bakst's lavish sets and exotic costumes in a riot of deep, rich colour. Patterned satin cushions with piping and tassels, and deep lampshades with long fringes, were part of the look. The corals, reds, Aztec green, jade green and an off-white usually associated with undyed wool were the influence of the

American Indians, while the golds and ochre derived from Ancient Egyptian art.

As the decade progressed, glitter and gloss invaded the home with lacquered furniture and screens, tiled floors, varnished walls and furniture, metallic paints and decorative objects in gold, silver, bronze, steel and chrome. Silver and black were a popular combination in interiors. The painters Van Gogh and Gauguin inspired bright colours and Eileen Gray showed screens lacquered in black, red and gold at the 1925 Paris exhibition.

At the end of the 1920s, Art Deco was giving way to Modernism. Accordingly, most fashionable interiors of the 1930s had low-key colour schemes based on neutrals like fawn, off-white, grey, with colour accents such as deep blue, coral or maroon. The overall lack of colour was offset by texture (from hand-woven fabrics and rugs) and sheen (from mirrors and glass). There was a vogue for monochrome rooms, based around a single colour such as sky blue, willow green, apricot, cyclamen or off-white. These were, however, almost always offset by accents in complementary colours. All-white rooms were also fashionable in the 1930s, and white or ivory satin evening dresses were in vogue too. This was followed by a general return to colour, including "shocking pink', which was introduced by the dress designer Elsa Schiaparelli.

American Interiors

The United States was a world leader in architecture in the 1920s, with such innovators as Frank Lloyd Wright and Raymond Hood. Indeed, the skyscrapers which were beginning to appear on the horizon are regarded by many as the country's greatest architectural achievement. Yet America felt it was so limited in the decorative arts at that time that it did not exhibit at the 1925 Paris Exposition (the exhibition which gave Art Deco its name).

American interiors were following much the same development as English rooms by this time. The century began with a growing desire to reduce clutter. Various style revivals had, as in England, led to antiques for the wealthy and reproductions for the more modest homes. The fashion for Art Deco (also called the Moderne style in the United States) in the 1920s included many design motifs that were noticeably inspired by the North and Central American Indians, especially the Aztecs and Navajos. The elegant minimalism of Modernism/the International style, which was also known as Streamline-modern in the United States, dominated fashionable American interiors of the 1930s. Modernism, in fact, remained the most dominant influence until the 1960s, when interest in it began to wane.

Meanwhile, America's textile manufacturing industry had developed apace, so that by World War I in this industry too the United States was the world leader.

CURTAINS AND DRAPERY

There seemed to be two schools of thought at this time – conservationism vs. Modernism. The former stuck fairly firmly with pre-World War I decoration, in which the Adam revival predominated and the look was very traditional, while the latter subscribed to a much simpler, more pared-down look, for which the window curtains were either simply headed and hung on tracks or hung underneath a plain pelmet box.

The development of the Art Deco style brought more imaginative use of ornament, but window treatments were, on the whole, fairly plain and simple. Beds too were more streamlined, and trimmings were fairly low-key. After the heady excitements of the previous century, it seemed that the curtain was destined to play a very secondary role in interior decoration.

At the turn of the century, window treatments had become considerably lighter, though pelmets were still an important feature. The 17th century influence is very evident in these French curtains *c.*1905, with their deep, ornamented pelmets. The blinds and holdbacks retain a Victorian feel.

Beds and Bed Hangings

Bedsteads were available in wood, iron and brass in almost every style. French-style drapery was very fashionable. Harrods were selling a neo-Louis Seize bed drapery where the bedstead could be moved without disturbing the drapery. Festoon valances on a plain lath, often with a goblet heading that pulled up on a cord, were a fashionable option. Heal's were broadening their market at the beginning of the century with "new bedsteads for epileptic patients (also supplied to the West Sussex and Kent lunatic asylums)" and later with a nice line in emergency beds for hotels for the Coronation of George V.

In the 1920s, early 18th century Spanish carved beds were a source of inspiration while the '30s and '40s were swayed by Hollywood glamour, with buttoned headboards and silver satin bedspreads.

In this 1927 interior, full frilled cutains are used not only at the windows but also around the recess where the bed is placed, creating a more intimate and private area within the room.

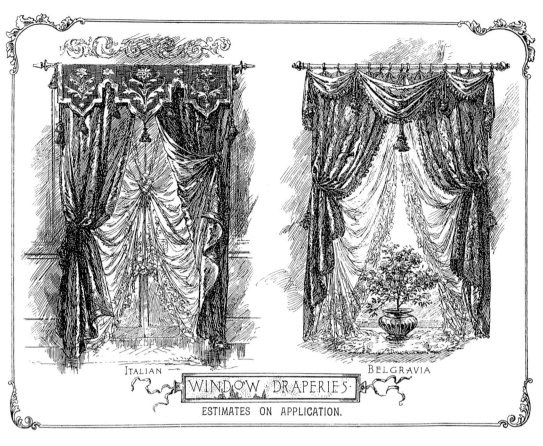

ITALIAN · WINDOW DRAPERIES · BELGRAVIA

ESTIMATES ON APPLICATION.

INSIDE BLINDS.

DUCHESS BLIND.   WINDOW   FESTOON BLIND.   BLINDS   LACE & INSERTION BLIND.

STRIPED TICK BLIND.   VENETIAN BLIND.   ART PRINTED BLIND.

Windows

Metal frames were one of the innovations of the 1920s–'30s. Traditional windows were updated with metal framing, squared bays, glass louvres and the like. Round shapes were fashionable such as portholes and windows with the glass rounded at the corners in the "suntrap" style.

Decorative frosting was popular, and patterns ranged from geometric to plant and animal motifs. Traditional features included dormers, leaded lights and the Queen Anne style wood-framed sash windows with thick, white-painted glazing bars and small panes of glass. Windows in suburban houses often had coloured glass with sunray, galleon or bird motifs or clear glass divided into rectangular panels with a small central casement.

Curtains

At this time the emphasis on fresh air, increased outdoor activities, simpler clothes and more freedom all influenced the style of window treatments. Bungalows, cottages and flats, as well as casement windows, made simpler, less expensive, treatments a necessity. By the 1920s the luxurious and complex ideas of the 19th century had almost completely disappeared.

Heal's deemed casement windows popular enough to warrant the development of a special fabric for casement curtains and blinds, known as casement flax. This advertisement is from their 1905 catalogue.

HEAL. & SON'S SPECIALITIES
FOR CASEMENT CURTAINS
Casement Flax,   36 in. wide, 1/3 to 1/9 yd.
Casement Cloths, 52 in. wide, 1/9 to 3/6 yd.
Casement Cottons, 32 & 52 in. wide, 8d. & 1/1 yd.

PATTERN BOOKS OF CRETONNES, CHINTZES OR CASEMENT MATERIALS SENT POST FREE ON APPLICATION

Opposite above: These examples of traditional treatments from Harrods' 1910 catalogue have overtones of Italian and Louis XV styles.

Opposite below: Blinds were very popular in the Edwardian period, and Harrods offered a wide range. These interior blinds from their 1910 catalogue were smart, elegant and well-detailed.

HELIOSCENE
BLIND.

ORIENTAL BLIND.

BOXHEAD
ROLLER BLIND.

Above and opposite: The exterior blinds from Harrods' 1910 catalogue were varied and original and designed to protect interior furnishings from strong sunlight.

At the very turn of the century, however, most households still favoured a traditional look, which could embrace a number of styles. Harrods' catalogue carried designs for Empire style, Louis Seize, Adam, Oriental, Italian, Louis Quinze and Elizabethan as well as typical Victorian drapery for bay windows, pianos, chimneys and beds.

Blinds were much in use, including festoon blinds in silk and roller blinds in linen union or Holland linen, often with lace insertions and sometimes printed with fashionable designs. The roller blinds, whether straight or shaped at the base, were always fringed to match. Painted, stained or varnished Venetian blinds were another option. Heal's announced "a new material" – casement flax – which it described in glowing terms:

> The casement curtain, or curtain blind, as it is sometimes called, which is now taking the place of the old-fashioned Venetian blind or spring roller blind, recommends itself on account of its decorative effect, in which respect the old blinds were sadly wanting. The want of a material which would drape well in the short length demanded by the casement curtain, and which at the same time was not expensive, has led us to the production of Casement Flax, which although pure linen, is not harsh, but always hangs in soft folds; it wears well and washes well, and great care has been exercised in selecting the fastest dyes, only those being used which had withstood severe tests of strong sunlight.

Harrods too carried designs for casement blinds, regarding which it offered the following advice:

> Casement blinds are decidedly the most convenient and picturesque form of blind for such windows. The upper short curtain (used of course only where there are transom or upper lights) should run on a pulleyed railway rod, fitted with eyes for hooks sewn on the curtains. The lower, except for exceptionally high windows, are made with rings to run on small brass or steel bronzed rods. A great improvement to the longer curtain is a "turnover" valance made about a fourth of its length and finished with a fringe. If a very long curtain is used it is better for one or two horizontal strips of lace appliqué. Shantung [an undyed wild silk] is the best material for Blind Curtains, forming a very effective shade against glare and falling in exquisite folds. Linen made with a specially soft finish is also much used, as are different types of Wool Challis.

Exterior blinds were an important feature of the period. Harrods carried a great variety, including outside Venetian blinds, "tropical" sun blinds made to reef or roll up, shutter or jalousie blinds for keeping rooms cool, helioscene blinds which afforded freedom of view and at the same time excluded the sun, box-head roller blinds and the strangely curving Oriental blinds.

Harrods clearly felt that not enough care was being taken with window treatments:

> It is quite usual, in an otherwise finely designed scheme of an interior for even the best architects and draughtsmen to indicate by a few lines or by a

wash of colour, the fact that a pair of curtains is intended for the window or the doorway, and the furnishing drapery department of a large business is generally supposed to be capable of dispensing with the services of a designer. This state of things Harrods Ltd. are taking every care to avoid by the co-ordination of their different furnishing departments and by every consideration being shown to the general surroundings. Clients may therefore be assured not only of a choice from an immense stock of fabrics of the finest designs and colourings but of the best artistic advice as to their application.

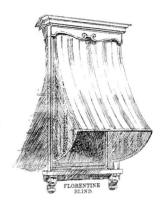

FLORENTINE BLIND.

There was also an interesting reference to seasonable decoration: "When the heavy curtains are taken down for the summer months, an effective decoration is to drape the pole with silk or some soft material, tying the lace curtains with sashes of the same colour, the pole rings being, of course, first removed."

The purported remark of a salesman to a concerned customer, that "taste is what you like", was sometimes stretched to the limit at this time, not least by the new novelty curtains. These included a variety of nets, gauze frilled with *point d'esprit*, and panel curtains in Nottingham, Brussels or Swiss appliqué lace, which began to supplement elaborately patterned laces.

The popular cottage-style window needed a different approach, and designers and department stores produced special materials and designs for the purpose. Goblet pleats remained a favourite heading, and there was a preoccupation with the problem of "deadlight" – the space between the top of the window architrave and the ceiling cornice. Harrods suggested "a piece of drapery hung from behind the pole, which is fixed as high above the top of the window as may be desired to add to the apparent light of the window, the valance being sufficiently deep to hide the window frame".

OUTSIDE VENETIAN BLIND.

Festoon blinds were usually recommended for sash windows, especially for rooms decorated in 18th century French or English styles. A wide range of poles, rods and pelmet boxes was available, with the pelmet boxes usually painted white or stained mahogany, oak or walnut.

During World War I fabric prices started to rise and in the ensuing years there was a great shortage of materials and the emergence of a quieter, more homely style of curtaining, though period styles were still admired. Flower prints or glazed cottons were popular, and plain curtains were given a richer look in colour and fabric. Velvets, slub silks or brocades were used in yellowy gold, royal blue or wine red and swathed in the 19th century styles as an alternative to the pelmet boards or stiffened pelmets.

SPANISH BLIND.

Curtained cupboards for bedrooms were a way of maximizing space in new smaller, post-war homes. Bed covers and curtains were usually in a matching fabric. The '20s and '30s saw a continuation of this pared-down look, the most usual curtain treatment being straight-hung paired curtains under a pelmet box. There were, however, some

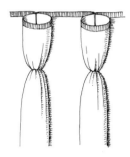

Goblet-pleat headings became fashionable in the Victorian era and have remained in vogue in the 20th century. The padded, cup-shaped pleats make a particularly attractive heading for a curtain or pelmet.

There is a strong Oriental feel about this 1927 Viennese design. The cross-over curtains have a smart red pelmet box, but in front of these the room is divided by a fabric-covered beam and pier from which an upholstered swing is suspended.

innovative ideas, such as a heraldic banner on a swing bracket. Some catalogues were showing the same decorative ideas they had been using for the last three decades.

The portière came back into fashion and appeared in a wide variety of fabrics including tapestries, velvets, brocatelles, damasks, plush, plain and figured velours, poplin, fancy reps, taffeta, chintz, dimity, cretonnes and even denim. Appliqué in leather or embroidery on plain fabric was popular, and tapestry panels were used for libraries and studies. Most curtains were straight and braided or bordered, but some unusual headings such as chain pattern were in vogue.

In general, the freedom of interpretation of past styles paved the way for a modern style of furnishing and decoration, but the somewhat debatable success of original designs in the first part of the 20th century kept people faithful to tradition to a large extent.

Fabrics

New techniques, fibres and dyes helped to modernize the textile industry in the early 20th century, and there were many changes and developments in the manufacture of fabrics. The emphasis shifted to easy care and hygiene. Man-made fibres, where natural fibres are regenerated and chemically treated, were introduced, proving resistant to shrinking and creasing and with less absorbency than natural cloths. Synthetic fibres, which were completely chemically derived, were developed as a cheaper substitute for natural fibres and, as techniques improved, they offered a much wider choice in price and quality.

Popular fabrics of the early 20th century included simplified versions of 18th-century patterns (used for both printed and woven fabrics) and designs based on 16th and 17th century needlework patterns. Plain fabrics were also found in many 1930s interiors.

In the early part of the century the French painter Raoul Dufy designed blockprinted textiles with geometric patterns inspired by Cubism, and in the '30s many other artist-inspired fabrics came on the market.

Typical Art Deco motifs were bold and flat, the pattern flamboyant and the sharp bursts of colour influenced by the colours of Matisse and the other Fauves, as well as the Ballets Russes. Orange and black, and blue and gold were two of the most popular colour combinations.

Trimmings

Trimmings did not change radically. Both the Art Deco and, particularly, the Modernist styles demanded less ornamentation. Braids were straight with mainly geometric motifs and they became smaller and neater as the century progressed. Fan-edged gimps and picot braids with patterns of small loops were frequently used. Fringes were deep-headed, often with crochet work with long bunches of fringe for the skirt. Tassels were generally smaller than in previous centuries. The heads were cylindrical or dome-shaped and the fringes corded, giving a gentle and graceful effect. An unusual and stylish variation to tassel heads was to have them made from cut-glass. Tie-backs often had superimposed chinoiserie motifs.

8

THE MID TO LATE 20TH CENTURY

The Country House Look and New Directions

World War II halted a boom period for architects and designers that had lasted for two decades. Since then, interior design has become a profession requiring technical knowledge combined with creativity and flair; a designer now needs to be able to tackle every aspect of an interior.

In post-war Britain there was an acute housing shortage, which continued until well into the 1950s. One solution was the building of prefabricated temporary homes, some of which still remain today. Permanent homes were built to a simple design with large windows. As building boomed again, it was the well-tried and tested styles such as mock-Tudor and neo-Georgian that tended to dominate. Many of the ugly space-saving tower blocks built in the '60s have proved unworkable in human terms, but the '80s and early '90s have seen exciting developments in modern architecture and some highly imaginative conversions of old buildings. No simple dominant style has developed, however, though each decade has shown some very recognizable elements.

In this unsettled, highly paced modern world, the nostalgia for a gentler, more gracious lifestyle is reflected in the chintz-covered interiors of the "Country House" look so popular in recent years. Pluralism and diversity have characterized the experimental Postmodern period. Colour and variety have once more become important elements in architecture, in contrast to the austerity and regularity of Modernism. The period has seen a return to some of the classical disciplines and historical forms and shapes. But with the approach of the year 2000 there are signs of new and exciting directions. Spaces are being opened up, lighting is playing a crucial role and functionalism is seen as something beautiful in its own right. The emphasis is now on quality of design and craftsmanship, while at the same time taking full advantage of the latest technology.

There is a nostalgic feel to this country bedroom with its flowered wallpaper and fabric, rugs and flowers. Simple curtains slotted on to swing brackets make an attractive solution to curtaining the recess.

Homes of the 1950s were designed to reflect people's increasingly informal lifestyles. Larger windows appeared in houses built then, flooding interiors with light, and stronger colours appeared in the new furnishing fabrics. The striped pelmet over sheers and matching portière curtains unify this interior.

INFLUENCES

In 1951 the Festival of Britain acted as a catalyst for the revival of British design consciousness and boosted British exports.

In the '60s Liberty's promoted the exciting new textile designers such as David Whitehead. Fabric was produced that was inspired by earlier periods (such as William Morris prints from the late 19th century) with the colouring adapted to 1960s taste. The neo-Art Deco mixed with Art Nouveau-style interior of Biba's short-lived department store in London inspired many contemporary homes with a softer, more nostalgic look. Laura Ashley began designing and selling simple, country-inspired smocks and dresses in small Victorian prints, and then built on this success to move into the home furnishing business with coordinated fabrics, wallpapers and paints. These were very affordable and made home decorating simple.

David Hicks was arguably the most influential designer of the time, producing an entirely new look with a highly successful mix of old and new styles, layouts sympathetic to modern needs, unusual wall-coverings and almost always distinctive geometric-patterned carpets.

Geometic patterns were much used by top designers in the '60s and '70s. The small pattern on this roman blind makes an effective backdrop for the strong lines of the modern chair.

Another major influence at this time was Terence Conran, whose chain of Habitat shops provided good-quality, clean-lined furniture along with attractive furnishings and accessories at very reasonable prices. The Conran look, like that of Laura Ashley, had a classless quality about it.

In the 1970s and '80s the influence of the 1920s and '30s was evident, with plain cream walls with a peach tint, Art Deco styles and geometric designs in soft shades for the curtaining. A high-glamour look was fashionable too, with festoon blinds, cream and gold colour schemes and fur bedcovers.

Perhaps, however, this period will be best remembered for the "Country House" style with an (often newly created) look of faded gentility, easy elegance, good furniture from different periods, chintz and clutter. This was inspired most of all by the work of John Fowler and his successors at Colefax and Fowler. Although the style had been

becoming increasingly popular ever since the 1930s, it was in the early 1980s when its popularity peaked and it was actually accepted as part of mainstream decoration.

LIFESTYLE

In the 1940s, during and after World War II, life was tough. Previous fashions seemed ugly and ridiculous. There was obviously no question of redoing a house or room; it was enough just to have escaped the bombing. Furniture was only made by government-approved manufacturers so it was basic and utilitarian. Despite the difficulties, many resourceful women produced delightful and individual homes. Walls were usually in a single colour wash and the furniture a mix of period and modern pieces, usually made in light wood. There was a vogue for stripping mid-Victorian chairs and tables for a lighter look. Carpet was hard to come by but felting in various colours was readily available. Accessories were used as a source of colour, with vivid cushions, baskets of flowers or plants, and groups of prints.

During and after World War II fashion was affected by rationing in the same way as interior decorating was. The government ordered manufacturers to produce utility clothes using as little fabric as possible.

The lack of servants and the new informality prompted a change in design in new homes. The living and dining areas were often combined to allow room for a better-planned kitchen; or, alternatively, there was a good-sized living room and a kitchen/diner. The upstairs usually consisted of two bedrooms, a box room and one bathroom.

With the post-war austerity years behind it, the mass consumer society began to take shape in the 1950s. Homes were now much more comfortable and layouts were linked to the new casual and informal lifestyle. Open-plan layouts allowed a housewife to cook and still remain near her husband, children and friends. These layouts gave a feeling of space and light, and windows were an important feature. Heating and insulation were increasingly efficient.

Two-colour effects were used on walls and furniture, wallpapers were mainly patterned, and harlequin patterns appeared underfoot. Fabrics were bright, with motifs such as sunfaces, stylized flower or leaf shapes, and small geometric patterns. Types of fabric were limited, however, with simple cotton twills, poplins and linens with slub or hopsack weaves. Floor-coverings were particularly important in the '60s, and wall-to-wall carpet was fashionable. So too were polished wood and cork with tufty cream or bleached fur rugs. Styles were often mixed, and walls were kept soft as a background for collections of paintings or groups of prints. Fabrics were often in soft pastel tones, with small, flowery Victorian designs used a great deal. Abstract designs were now based on technology rather than traditional patterns.

The Country House look has been widely used to soften city rooms. Here, the curtains are generously frilled, small tables are covered with fabric and sofas heavily fringed.

As the pace of life increased, city life grew more stressful and it became fashionable to have a second home in the country. Many old houses and cottages were renovated at this time.

Modern interiors became more elegant and mature in creamy beiges, with silk or linen walls and large sofas in suede or leather or cream upholstery fabrics. Good lighting, the coffee table and tablescapes also became important features. Eastern influence brought in rugs, tented ceilings and floor level day beds with cushions and incense. The well-off older generation still furnished with antiques or good reproduction furniture, deeply swathed curtains and plushy upholstery or slubbed silks and brocades.

A design from the 1950s, showing an innovative dining area with striped canopy above, continuous café curtains forming a backdrop and a cushion-covered divan. A variety of patterns and colours have been used; the orange and turquoise were particularly popular for fabrics of the time.

Futuristic interiors using perspex, coloured plastic and tubular metals started to appear, showing a close parallel to the modernistic developments of the late '20s. In contrast, the country style was also popular, with patchwork quilts, brass bedsteads and stripped pine representing something of a reaction to the brashness of the '60s.

In the 1970s and '80s, when property was one of the best forms of investments, home extensions and improvements were very popular. Professional and amateur renovations were a fast growth area, and a new individuality was stamped on interiors. Major advances in lighting played an important part in this.

Other countries have handled design developments with varying degrees of success. In France and Italy the period architecture of many cities has been well preserved, and Italian designers have been very successful at creating modern interiors within stylized period buildings. In France modern design and architecture are actively encouraged, but period buildings are handled with great sympathy. Recently the "provençal" or French provincial style has had

Tied-back sheer curtains create a theatrical frame for two green roller blinds and a central cream blind with an orange-tree design, in this imaginative country bedroom.

international appeal, with adaptations of it appearing in towns as well as countryside across Europe and America.

The United States has been at the forefront of 20th century design, with the emphasis more on the planning of space and use of materials than on surface decoration. America's leading designers have been highly influential. Sister Parish and Albert Hadley are a prime example of a design practice which has not only excelled at planning and layout but has effectively used the best of the past within a modern context. Marietta Gomez creates functional rooms as a background to art, antiques and handicrafts. Bill Blass produces sleek, edited interiors, and Mark Hampton and David Anthony Easton both take their inspiration from the 18th century. John Saladino, who popularized the aged and distressed look, favours an unusual palette with colours such as violet, amethyst and celadon green, and often uses overscaling to add drama to his interiors. Although all these designers work in different styles they, like their European counterparts, strive to achieve a quality of interior design that is not only beautiful but really works for the people who live and work within it.

Furniture and Upholstery

Having become increasingly unfashionable, the three-piece suite has been replaced to a large extent by a combination of sofas and occasional, arm and wing chairs, in various shapes and sizes. Run-offs and pouffes are often included for extra seating cum coffee tables.

Although Adam and Regency style dining-chairs have remained popular, an alternative has been high-backed upholstered chairs, which blend happily with most styles. Where space is limited, built-in bench

Interior designer Derek Frost often designs his own furniture. Form and colour play a vital part, and there is a great feeling of movement in his work.

seats, particularly in kitchen/dining-rooms, have been a good solution; they are often banked with cushions for colour and decoration. There have been some exciting developments in furniture design and it has become increasingly fashionable to commission special pieces.

Colours

Bright colours were popular during World War II, perhaps as a morale booster. The American architect Frank Lloyd Wright liked to use colours sympathetic to the actual building materials and developed a brick red that was particularly associated with his work.

There was a note of optimism in the colours of the '50s. The fashion designer Jacques Fath set a trend with a shade known as hot pink. Strong colours appeared in the new fabric designs such as orange, pistachio, red, pink, kingfisher blue and turquoise. There was also a softer range inspired by the palette of the Scandinavian designers.

Strong colours and bold design in a fabric by Nina Campbell create an inviting corner in a sitting room. Even the books fit into the colour scheme.

A neo-Edwardian feel in this pretty sitting room is achieved with pastel colours, chintz loose covers and countrified furniture.

In the '60s there were ethnic and Oriental influences. Very cheap and brightly coloured cottons and an ever widening range of new synthetic fabrics and new dyes were features of the period. Floors and walls were often in brilliant colours and murals and wallhangings were commonly used.

The '70s was the era of coordination. Many manufacturers now offered a whole range of coordinating fabrics, wallpapers, borders, etc. Brown and cream, and avocado and gold were popular colour combinations. The "high tech" look which was also fashionable at this time had no indigenous colour; walls were painted or left plain.

As a reaction to high tech, an Edwardian revival developed, with soft, gentle tints of peach, coral, light greens or yellow and understated patterns of traditional flower, leaf and trellis motifs. This was dominant in the '80s, though the classic elegance of creams and beiges was far from forgotten.

American Interiors

In 1947 *House & Garden* magazine published "A Complete Guide to Interior Decoration", which highlighted the contrast between America and Europe. Although austerity was lifting in Britain by the end of the 1940s, America's styles were more sophisticated than their British counterparts. At this time the United States favoured the Federal and Colonial styles, with late 18th and early 19th century antique or reproduction furniture combined with striped wallpaper and appropriate mirrors and curtaining. There was also a Scandinavian style featuring colourful upholstery in a tweed or linen weave for textural interest, bright curtains and one of the four walls often painted a rich, intense colour such as chocolate brown or olive green.

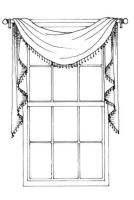

This swagged drapery is representative of more sophisticated Early American treatments.

Roughly paralleling the development of the Country House look in England was America's Early American style. Since the last quarter of the 19th century, the interest in Americana had been growing in the United States, along with an enthusiasm for country furniture, old pine, rag rugs, patchwork quilts and folk art. This was also fuelled by the Crafts Revival, which began in the United States in the 1950s, partly due to the influx of craftsmen trained at the Bauhaus. The Early American style brings together all these aspects, and is characterized by Colonial-style furniture, much use of chintzes (the popularity of which did not die out this century in America as it did for a while in England), ginghams, plaids and stripes, small-scale calico prints and muslin, along with a prevalence of ruffles, scallops and piping. Antiques and modern items are cheerfully mixed in a way that is uniquely 20th century.

The Country House look is also popular in America, though, broadly speaking, it is interpreted there in more adventurous colourways. Colour preferences remain one of the fundamental differences in approach between the two countries, with England generally holding to soft, muted tones and America tending to prefer stronger, brighter colours.

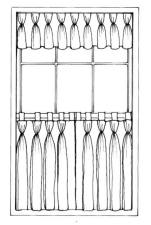

Café curtains with a valance are widely used in Early American window treatments. These are goblet-pleated and hung from the pole with fabric tapes.

CURTAINS AND DRAPES

The second half of the century saw a much more imaginative approach to window treatments. In the '50s the emphasis seemed to be on the actual fabrics but by the '60s there were a number of different style revivals. Finally, however, the Country House style seemed to be the most definitive; bed and window curtains became the focal point of the room once again, with ornately draped pelmets and valances,

OVERLEAF:
A charmingly dressed full-tester bed and matching window treatment. The softly pleated and shaped valance is lined in pink to match the flowers on the main fabric and edged in a deeper pink for definition. The curtains are given a similar treatment, and softly draped sheers, also in pink, are just visible behind them.

contrasting linings and lavish trimmings. As in the 19th century, there was an inevitable reaction to a surfeit of drapery, and a new emphasis on simplicity and high quality has emerged. The latest styles owe much to some of the earliest forms of curtaining.

Beds and Bed Hangings

The Country House style has seen the revival of elaborate bed treatments, including the fully dressed full-tester, the half-tester and variations on the corona, all of which give tremendous scope for imaginative use of fabrics, linings and trimmings.

French-style beds have enjoyed considerable popularity, sometimes featuring simple drapery trailing over the ends of the bed and sometimes left quite plain, with the emphasis on the elegant shape and interesting grain of the wooden head and foot boards.

Brass bedsteads and patchwork quilts are used in cottage style interiors. However, the general trend, in sympathy with the latest window treatments, is more streamlined, with the bed treated as an integral part of the scheme rather than as an eye-catching centrepiece.

The half-tester bed is less overpowering than a full-tester (four-poster) but still allows for imaginative use of fabric, linings and trimmings.

Windows

Windows have, on the whole, continued to grow in size since the 1950s. The trend has been to bring the outside in and give an interior as much light as possible.

Windows are often designed to frame a view. Windows on sliding runners hung from ground to ceiling level are still popular, forming a virtually transparent screen between the interior and exterior.

Whereas in the earlier part of the century windows had mainly been made of metal, during the latter half there was a return to wood, particularly when the early metal windows had problems with condensation.

These days windows are available in almost any shape, size or style including skylights, but the Georgian sash is still the most popular.

Curtains

World War II saw curtain and chair-cover materials rationed, though special allocations were sometimes granted. The housewife was often left with the choice of clothes or furnishing. Mattress ticking, duster material and even dyed parachute silk were pressed into service, reappearing as attractive curtains. Countrified printed cottons with flowers and trellis were popular and complemented the mix of old and new furnishings. Secondhand materials were often dyed to fit a scheme. Deep shades such as wine red, pine green or golden brown were the most successful dyes and went with the look that was then popular. Where there was enough fabric available, tie-backs were added. Department stores also offered ready-made curtains in the 1940s. Harrods carried "Florida Frilled Curtains ready for immediate fitting with a slot for rod and heading . . . specially made to fit modern windows". The curtains, which had frills on both sides and at the bottom, were made in marquisette that was either plain or had coloured tufts of green, peach, rose, gold, red, blue, brown or natural on a cream ground.

There were no great innovations in curtain design in the 1950s and '60s. Plain or shaped box pelmets combined with straight-hung curtains were the most usual choice. Ready-made curtains, hemmed and headed with a gathered heading tape were an inexpensive option. Coordination was taken to the extreme: everything from curtains through to table linen and tissue box could be coordinated.

An exciting variety of blinds have become available in recent years. Pleated blinds make a dramatic window treatment in their own right in this modern interior. The straight lines of the blind make a pleasing backdrop to the curved shapes of the chair and table in the foreground.

Venetian blinds became fashionable again and were now offered in different widths and an extensive colour range to match any decorative scheme. Strong and hardwearing, they were a good choice for use in offices. A variety of other blinds were also introduced, including blackout blinds to help children sleep or to allow the showing of slides, sun-filtering blinds and special blinds which give privacy by appearing opaque from the outside but which allow one to look out unhindered from the inside.

By the 1970s drapery was fashionable again as part of the English Country House neo-Edwardian/Victorian look. Curtains were made with much more fabric for a fuller look, and pelmets and valances were swagged, smocked, pleated and ruched, and decorated with fringes, rosettes and choux. Pull-up blinds, Austrian and festoon, enjoyed a renaissance until it seemed that every home in the land must have one.

As in previous centuries a reaction against this overstuffed look set in, and curtain design is now seen as a part of the whole scheme rather than the dominant part. In some cases, the very early style of curtaining is providing inspiration for window treatments. For lovers of beautiful things, however, the taste of the past has a nostalgic charm and attraction, which ensures a continuing tradition in period styles of bed and window drapery.

It is perhaps worth mentioning here that curtains are not merely confined to the home, office, shop or showroom. Theatre curtains too come in many different guises. They can be pulled up from the side on cords and pulleys, they can work on the same principle as Austrian or festoon blinds or they can roll up from the base rather like a roller blind in reverse. Where there is a very tall proscenium, fabric stretched on a frame can be raised and lowered like the lower half of a sash window.

Curtains appear too in somewhat unexpected places, such as museums, where they are used to protect delicate items like tapestries from damage by light. Exterior fabric decorations may also be a source of inspiration for the interior. Interlaced swags and festoons in patriotic colours can make a wonderful draped heading for sheer curtains, and a spray of swags an attractive central motif.

Fabrics

The department stores worked hard to stay abreast of current trends in fabric design and technology. In 1940 Harrods brought out "chintzaleen", which was described as "a new and delightful fabric that has the appearance of chintz but does not require glazing after cleaning"; it cost 3 shillings 6 pence a yard. Simple weaves such as gingham and other "utility" fabrics were characteristic of the 1940s. Another legacy of the war was the use of restricted colour schemes in fabric design, which in Britain lasted into the 1950s but did not occur in the United States. The majority of designs produced at this time used no more than two or three colours on a neutral grey, white or black background. Needlework patterns from the 16th and 17th centuries were popular sources of designs for woven and printed textiles, as indeed they had been ever since the 1920s.

The 1950s brought bold flowers, jazzy geometrics and abstract patterns, many of them inspired by the Festival Patterns created for the 1951 Festival of Britain by such designers as Lucienne Day. Science and technology were sources of inspiration, as in designs based, for example, on the structure of a crystal.

A chair becomes a feature in its own right when covered with this startling fabric designed by Cressida Bell.

In this bedroom decorated by Chester Jones, the cupboards are tied into the room by placing fabric to match the curtains behind the mesh on the cupboard doors. The pelmet is built out in a semi-circular shape for added interest.

Smaller patterns worked well with the new sophisticated interiors of the '60s. The clean, bright colours and simple, modern designs of Scandinavian fabrics from firms like Marimekko and Vuoko of Finland also became popular from about this time. Another influence on 1960s fabric prints came from art – specifically, pop art, op art and graphic design.

Patterns by William Morris and other Arts and Crafts designers also became popular again from this time, in both Britain and America. As the Country House look took hold, the huge revival of chintzes of every sort and description began.

The soft pastel designs of Tricia Guild for Designers Guild and simulated paint finishes from Osborne & Little gave the '70s a fresh new look. Ethnic textiles were also characteristic of this decade, as were the small-scale, one- and two-colour prints popularized by Laura Ashley. Showing similarly nostalgic origins was the growing demand in America for Americana designs, especially as a result of the 1976 Bicentennial celebrations.

In the 1980s the Country House look led to an interest in authenticity and faithfully reproduced "document fabrics", not only in the original colour but also in colourways more suited to modern tastes. Toiles de Jouy too became very popular once more. Other fabrics that were fashionable in the '80s were stripes, checks and plaids, ikat prints and weaves and flamestitch prints and weaves.

Fabric design has not become retrogressive, however, as there have been many innovations, such as Timney Fowler's striking black-and-white "architectural" designs with Classical motifs, Jane Churchill's range of fabrics featuring characters from Alice in Wonderland, Collier Campbell's and Manuel Canovas's exciting colour combinations and Celia Birtwell's fresh, modern fabrics. Brunschwig & Fils, the American fabric designers, have produced patterns reflecting a broad range of historical and geographical reference. A deeper, richer palette is currently desirable, and interiors have been given a pleasing patina with the addition of antique textiles made into cushions, used for upholstery or thrown over tables. Never has there been a wider or more exciting range to choose from.

Trimmings

The aesthetic benefits of trimmings are well understood these days, and there is an enormous variety to choose from, including exquisite handmade items much used in restoration and conservation work. The big comfy sofas and elaborately swagged curtains associated with the Country House look have been accompanied by deep bullion fringes, and braids and borders have been imaginatively used on leading edges or inset into the curtains. It is possible to have these trimmings made up in any combination of colours to match a decorative scheme and give a professional finish.

Delightful detailing to the base of a curtain with a deep contrasting checked border and bullion fringe. This is part of a room decorated by Roger Banks-Pye, a leading decorator at Colefax and Fowler.

The delicate all-over pattern used in this attic guest bedroom reflects John Fowler's love of France and is a good example of his use of pattern. The clever positioning of the corona allows the curtains to be draped at opposite corners of the bed.

9

Selecting Styles and Fabrics

There are many factors to take into account when selecting a style. The amount of wall space on either side of the window, or the headroom above it, is sometimes limited and will affect the approach to the curtaining. And, of course, the function of the room will have a bearing. Other factors might include the need to disguise an ugly outlook or, alternatively, to draw the eye to a beautiful view. Strong architectural features such as a heavy fireplace may need balancing, the amount of light coming in may be important and there are always the elements of mood and atmosphere to take into account.

A curtain treatment can be effectively used to improve proportions and balance in a room but fine architectural features should not be disguised by heavy swathes of fabric. Floor-length curtains appear to reduce floor space whereas curtains caught back or made to sill length make this look greater. In a small room, therefore, it is a good idea to tie curtains back. In any case, soft curtains usually look best when they are caught back. As spaces grow smaller, allowing little room for grand furniture, textiles are more valuable than ever for decorative effect.

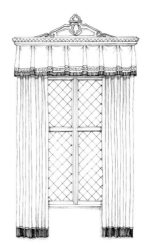

Drawing inspiration from French 16th century styles, a pleated fringed pelmet is surmounted by a cornice, from which hang three-quarter-length paired curtains. This treatment works especially well for mullion windows.

WINDOW SHAPES

The most important consideration of all before selecting any particular style of treatment is the shape of the window itself.

Timber-framed Mullioned Windows

Elegant blinds complement the furniture and fittings in this Regency-style dining room. The gold of the fabric is particularly pleasing against the rich wood and deep wall colourings. The blinds successfully soften the bay window, where curtain options are limited as the windows are so close together.

One of the major considerations with these windows, which were typical of 16th and early 17th century architecture, is the loss of light. Historically they would have had shutters, possibly sashes or maybe in the 17th century the most basic form of curtaining.

For modern purposes any treatment should be kept simple. Paired curtains on a pole would be suitable or, in a grander room, a French 16th-century-style treatment with a pleated, fringed pelmet underneath a cornice with three-quarter-length paired curtains.

Sash Windows

The sash window, more than any other, has become the hallmark of British architecture, though it has also been used extensively elsewhere, particularly in the United States. Associated especially with the 18th century, it is still a popular choice today.

In the 17th and 18th centuries, sash windows would probably have been dressed with elegant pull-up curtains that rested between the window architrave and ceiling cornice, leaving the architecture unimpaired and letting in the maximum amount of light. In the mid-18th century the French used elegant shallow pelmets with paired curtains, a look that would still work well today in a formal room, hall,

A design from Susan Llewellyn Associates for a newly married couple on a tight budget. A panel of rich, strong fabric is inset at the top of plain paired curtains, which are then caught back with the same patterned fabric. This is a wonderful way to use a piece of antique fabric picked up in an antique shop or market.

Opposite: When choosing curtain fabric, don't forget to take into account the trimmings, which can play an important role in the overall look. Here, bold tassels suspended by cords from fabric chou match the fringe and help to emphasize the dramatic outline.

202

The Regency period was notable for drapery, deep pelmets or valances, ornate curtain poles and lavish trimmings and borders, all features which can be used to evoke a period feel, particularly on sash windows.

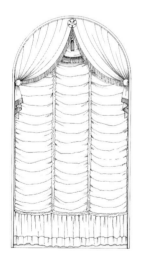

A store marquise makes an attractive treatment in its own right and provides a good way to treat an arched window. Combined with paired curtains and executed in a fine silk or similar fabric, it can provide an excellent screen for an unattractive view.

library or study. Towards the end of the century pelmets were swagged and side curtains caught back.

In the Regency period asymmetrical drapery was fashionable, and those elegant styles can be successfully adapted for modern rooms.

A late 19th century idea was to frame the window with a lambrequin and use a blind to exclude light.

Top-heavy pelmet treatments should be avoided. The window can be made to seem wider by using generous curtains with the heading meeting in the middle. With these long, narrow windows, floor-length curtains look best in order not to spoil the proportions.

Attic Dormers

These pose some practical problems as the space available for hanging is usually limited. Early attic dormers were part of the servants' quarters and would probably have been fitted with shutters.

For curtains, a track or slim pole can usually be fitted within the side walls of the dormer, close against the window. Or curtains can be slotted onto a hinged rod(s), so they can be swivelled open to rest against the dormer wall during the day. Sheers can be threaded onto narrow rods at the top or bottom of the window itself.

If there is generous headroom above the window a pole could be placed the width of the window suspending paired curtains, which would then be caught back against the sloping wall with thin rods.

Venetian and Arch-headed Windows

Venetian, or Palladian-style, windows were borrowed from the designs of the 16th century Venetian architect Andrea Palladio and became a feature of Palladian-revival architecture in the early 18th century. Variations of the Venetian window have been used ever since. Thomas Chippendale introduced a special curved curtain cornice from which swags were suspended over the central section and the straight cornice was placed over the side windows for the tails. The whole effect was to soften the architecture.

Arched windows have been treated in a number of different ways through the centuries. In the 17th and 18th centuries, curved-headed, ornamented lambrequins were combined with paired curtains caught back in rope tie-backs.

"Store marquise", a light, clear, heavily festooned blind, was sometimes combined with a fixed heading of drapery. Another option was a similarly fixed swagged heading secured within the arch, with tails of fabric at each side of the window and the addition of a roller blind.

Italian strung, or reefed, curtains, which were caught back one-third of the way down, allowed in the maximum amount of light. Their heading remained fixed and they would be raised and lowered to the side on a cord system rather like theatre curtains. These days curved

Sunray pleating on an arched Colonial-style transom gives an original effect if light is not a priority.

In this room, by Fine Art Interiors, a fixed-head treatment for these Gothic windows, with the curtains caught back quite high up, allows the maximum amount of light into the room. To close the curtains the tie-backs would simply be removed.

track is available to make fitting easier, and so curved-headed curtains or blinds can be used.

Where space allows, a pole or track can be placed above the window so the curtains can be hung clear of the window on either side. This is a good solution for Gothic-shaped windows.

Where the arched windows are tall and the proportions allow, a curved lambrequin could be combined with Italian-strung curtains.

A small arched window can look delightful with just a patterned or decorated lambrequin, with a roller blind behind if blackout is required. If the window is Gothic-shaped, the lambrequin could be cut to complement the outline of the window. An 18th century device was to paint the blind with heraldic designs to simulate stained glass.

Arched windows are often found in quite formal rooms, where stylish fabrics such as brocades, damasks and silks look particularly effective.

A Colonial-style transome can be attractively decorated with a "sunburst" curtain if light is not of prime importance.

A lambrequin makes a charming treatment for an arched window. Here, the strong pattern has been carefully matched for maximum effect.

French Windows

There are a variety of effective ways that French windows can be treated. The simple Louis XIV style with sculpted, stiffened pelmet/lambrequin is one option. Another possibility is the Victorian adaptation of this, with generous curtains caught back on cloak pins and panels of sheer fabric or lace attached to the top and bottom of the window by wire rods.

The late 19th century style of scarf drapery combined with roller blinds if blackout is required is a stylish option.

A pair of plain roller or Roman blinds where the windows are recessed and there is no wallspace available for curtains would solve the problem. If desired, the blinds could be patterned and highly decorative and even dressed with their own mini-lambrequin.

Thomas Sheraton designed elegant treatments of swagged headings with the tails caught in bows at intervals and paired curtains tied back in cords in an attractive shape three-quarters of the way down and breaking on the floor.

In Ackermann's *Repository* a very tall French window has gentle swags hung from a decorative curtain cornice with central motif, combined with lightweight bordered, paired curtains caught back high up and an asymmetrical sheer also caught back to allow a clear passage through the door to the garden.

In larger houses several of these windows sometimes appear together on one wall. The Regency idea of linking them together with one continuous pelmet can be very successfully adapted, with either individual pairs of curtains for each window or a curtain at each end of the series of windows.

If the window is not really in use for access to garden or balcony, full-length paired curtains that meet in the centre with a pelmet or draped pelmet or with a pleated heading, look soft and pretty and can take a variety of trimmings and ornamentation.

When space is limited between window architrave and ceiling cornice, paired curtains on a pole with swagging attached look attractive by day and appear pelmeted by night when drawn.

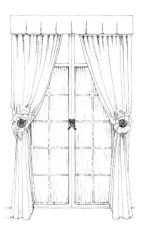

Full curtains caught back on cloakpins with a stiffened shaped pelmet give a traditional 19th century feel to these French windows.

Plain mini-lambrequins combined with fringed and patterned roller blinds provide an innovative solution to the problem of lack of wall space near French windows.

For windows with no space above the frame, swags and tails can be attached to the curtain itself.

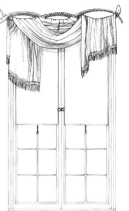

A striking effect achieved with modest elements. A strong-coloured roller blind is combined with scarf drapery over an unusual form of pole.

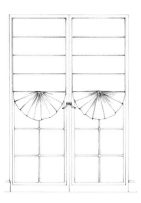

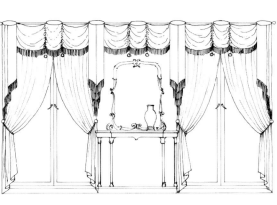

Left: An original idea with unlined Roman blinds. The base pulls up like a fan, and the absence of lining allows the light to shine through and the structure of the blind to become a feature in itself.

Right: Two or more windows on the same wall can be successfully linked with "continuous drapery" – using one pelmet or valance across both windows and the wall.

Opposite: A variation on a traditional treatment for these French windows. While the paired curtains are kept simple, the deep pelmet has a double trimming to add texture and interest.

A window seat works well within the recess created by a bay window. Here it is framed by a pair of curtains and an interestingly shaped pelmet, the line of which has been dictated by the pattern itself.

Pelmet boards built out in a semi-circular or rectangular shape, which was a Victorian idea, look pleasing and allow extra freedom of movement for the curtain. An interesting shape can also be created with curtain cornicing if there is space above the window and the proportions are treated with care.

Reefed curtains with a goblet-pleated heading or perhaps a swagged pelmet allow plenty of light into the room.

Bay Windows

Bay windows were a Victorian development following the removal of window tax and improvements in glass-making techniques. The corners of the bay can easily look awkward, which is why the Victorians favoured swags and tails that hid them well.

Where the window frames are light and the windows close together, a single pair of curtains on either side of the bay works well; the addition of a pelmet will soften the effect of the expanse of glass. However, where the frames are heavier and there is more available space between the windows, intermediate curtains look attractive. These can be caught back at different heights for different effects and can be combined with roller blinds in a matching or contrasting fabric.

Individual pull-ups above a built-in window seat make an elegant solution. If the pull-ups are too complex for regular use they can be combined with roller blinds.

A wide variety of tie-backs and hold-backs are available today. Wooden and brass hold-backs can be chosen with a motif that is sympathetic to the period of the window.

There are an enormous varierty of poles to choose from these days. The finials are particularly decorative features and if carefully chosen can add to the feeling of period.

Combined Windows and Glazed Doors or Two Windows Together

These generally look best when treated as a whole with a track or pole across the top of the door and window, extending a little beyond, with a pair of curtains suspended, one at each end and with a third in the centre. The curtains can be tied back or hung straight.

The track could be covered with a cornice (which should be narrow to allow the door to open and shut if it opens inwards) and unified with trimmings and blinds. An alternative might be to use only a pair of curtains and attach sheers or blinds to the front of the door and window.

As some of these window styles were typical of the Arts and Crafts Movement, the use of a dramatic, hand-blocked fabric would be a sympathetic choice.

This recessed cottage-style window has been framed with tied-back paired curtains and a shaped stiffened pelmet across the top.

A modern adaptation of the lambrequin combined with a blind makes a smart treatment in this hallway. A lambrequin like this has the additional advantage that it will cut out draughts.

Cottage-style Windows

These do not, as a general rule, look good with overly formal or dressy treatments. Pattern, weight of fabric and style should be carefully balanced, and three-quarter or sill-length curtains are often preferable as this makes the window seem deeper. If pelmets or drapery are to be used they should be kept well in proportion so they do not overpower the window itself.

As the possibilities for curtain styles are rather limited on these windows, the scope is really in the choice of fabric and imaginative use of borders and trimmings. The Edwardians were very fond of frogging on pelmets, and smocked headings can look delightful in a country bedroom.

Some older cottage-style windows are fitted with shutters, excellent barriers against crime, noise, cold and light in their own right. The shutters can be used on their own and, if liked, given a decorative paint treatment to make them more attractive when closed at night. Tall shutters could even be mirrored in the French 18th century style to reflect night lighting. Where the shutters are non-working, Roman or roller blinds could be fixed in the recess, or an adaptation of the 17th century sash could be fitted for privacy.

In order to hang curtains successfully, the pole or track would have to be extended well beyond the shutters on either side of the window to give shutters freedom of movement or allow the shutters to be seen. For the same reason, any pelmet or draped heading would need to be shallow if the shutters are working.

Casement Windows

In the 1920s and '30s many department stores carried special "casement" fabrics and styling suggestions in their catalogues.

Wide windows of any sort are difficult to treat successfully, and often these appear overdressed and rather like a stage set. Without double glazing they can be a serious source of draughts, so it is advisable to extend the track or pole well beyond the frame, where wall space allows, to prevent this. Unless there is a window sill, floor-length curtains look best, lined and interlined for insulation. Curtains that meet in the centre of the window at the top and are then tied back appear to reduce the window width, while softly shaped pelmets or draped headings reduce the impact. Harsh light or an unattractive view can be softened with sheers. Plain or textured fabric often works best – any pattern should be bold and clear. Flat blinds such as Roman or roller blinds in a plain fabric with a border for definition would look smart, but festoon or Austrian blinds should be avoided as they would look fussy on such wide windows.

Side-swinging Door or Window

The only possible solution for these is to use a blind or café curtains attached to the actual frame so that they move with the door or window.

Angled Windows

Angled windows were an innovation in suburban houses of the 1920s and '30s. The usual heading would have been a pelmet box with a curtain at each end of each window and two curtains together where the windows met. An alternative would be Roman blinds or Venetian blinds in a colour to tone with the decoration of the room.

Skylights

Sheer fabric anchored on rods at the top and bottom of the sloping window will diffuse the light, but if blackout is required a Venetian blind fixed at both ends of the frame, or Roman or roller blinds held with strategically placed rods, are options. Some "rooflights" can be fitted with blinds trapped between two layers of glass, making a neat double-glazed unit. The blind is controlled from below.

Skylights and rooflights are difficult to treat, but blinds are a good option with the addition of strategically placed rods to give extra support and prevent sagging.

Patio Doors and "Walls of Glass"

These are often best left as intended – that is, a virtually invisible barrier between interior and exterior – but where privacy or blackout is required the main problem is usually lack of wall space. Any form of pelmet would not only take away precious light but would impede the workings of the door. A French-pleated heading on track curved around to the adjoining wall would be a solution in keeping, especially if the fabric were kept plain and the trimmings simple, such as a border, piping or bound edges.

SELECTING FABRIC

These days every conceivable sort of fabric is available and the enormity of choice is sometimes overwhelming. Before any purchase is made, it is important to consider the way a fabric will be used, the type of wear it will be subjected to, the draping quality needed and the importance of easy care and cleaning. Each item of fabric in a scheme should be matched not only to the other fabrics in the room-design but also to the flooring, wallcovering, furniture and accessories. Sunlight and electric light can radically alter its appearance and colour, so it is important to look at a prospective fabric in both types of light and in the room for which it is intended. It should be held in the way it will be hung to see how well it drapes, and a variety of different trimmings should be held against it so that just the right weight and style can be chosen. It is often at this working stage that a really witty and original combination comes together.

Careful consideration should be given to mood and atmosphere, which are important elements in a scheme. For example, where something grand and formal is required, velvet, silk or damask might be appropriate, whereas a plain wool or simple checked cotton would suit an informal sitting-room. Also, think about how much light you will want to let into the room and whether it matters if the curtains diminish it. One of the most exciting elements of fabrics is the contrast of light and shade. Where reflected light is required in a scheme a fabric with a sheen would be suitable, while a dark, matt fabric would absorb light. The subtlety of soft pale tones will give interesting shadow when a room is lit at night, and textural contrasts add interest. It is worth noting that dark colours tend to look darker when hung at a window because of the contrast with the bright sunlight.

If fabric is likely to be exposed to strong sunlight, avoid silk, which is prone to fading unless it is lined, interlined, and, ideally, protected with a blind as well.

The function of a room will also influence the choice of fabric. Easy-care fabrics are obvious choices for kitchens where grease and steam pose a problem. Cotton is a good choice for bathrooms, as wool retains moisture and silk tears easily if wet. Tiles and equipment make for an excess of hard and shiny surfaces here, and the fabric provides a softening element.

Dress fabrics, often much cheaper than their home-furnishing counterparts, are, in the main, a temptation not to be succumbed to, as they are not intended to stand up to heavy wear-and-tear or be exposed to strong sunlight. Supposed budget fabrics can be deceptive, so it is advisable to give them a rub test before purchasing to make certain that a dressing, to give extra body, has not been applied. Colour variation can be a problem so fabric should ideally be bought from the same roll.

The actual weight of a fabric is relevant too. Many cotton or wool weaves are just too heavy to drape well for curtains. On the other hand, a heavy fabric with good draping qualities will hang in deep folds, giving a dramatic and voluptuous look. A medium to lightweight fabric would have a neater, more tailored appearance.

Fabrics do not, of course, have to be brand-new to be effective. Markets, antique shops and shops specializing in antique fabrics can be a wonderful source of the unusual for cushions, borders or even pairs of old curtains.

FABRIC FIBRES

There are three main categories of fibre for fabrics: natural, man-made and synthetic. Some fabrics, such as satin, corduroy and lace, can be made entirely of cotton, which is a natural fibre, but can also be made completely from man-made and synthetic yarns. Fabrics made from natural fibres are generally dirt-resistant and clean well. Man-made fabrics resist shrinkage and creasing and are less absorbent than natural cloths. Synthetics attract surface dirt and need more frequent washing, which can spoil the texture.

Natural Fibres

Natural fibres are constructed from vegetable and animal sources such as cotton, flax, wool and silk.

Cotton comes from cotton plants, is economic to produce and can be dyed at almost any stage. It is very versatile, with a wide range of weight and textures, and is tough, resilient and practical. Indian cotton is of fairly poor quality; Sea Island cotton is especially lustrous and silky.

Linen comes from flax and is less widely grown than cotton, more complex to produce and so more expensive. Lustrous, dirt-resistant and hardwearing, linen is often blended with other fibres, such as cotton, to make it more supple and cheaper; linen/cotton union is one example. It is ideal for tailored coverings, or formal, lined and interlined floor-length curtains, as its weight gives it heavy folds. It tends to crease easily, however.

Silk, from silkworms, is the finest, smoothest and strongest natural fibre. It accepts dye well and drapes beautifully. It is often mixed with wool, or linen for durability, and is best not stretched taut, on cushions for example. There are cheap, lightweight Indian or Chinese silks, while Thai silk is the most beautiful and the most expensive.

Wool comes in many different types, according to the breed of sheep it derives from. Wool's warmth comes from the protein structure of fibres and the "crimp" that hold air between them. Combing produces a smooth yarn and carding a fluffy yarn. Wool is warm and comforting and drapes softly and well. It is often blended with other fibres, particularly linen or silk for use in soft furnishings. Manufacturing processes have reduced the risk of shrinkage.

Man-made Fibres

These are natural fibres which have been regenerated from natural materials and chemically treated.

Acetate and viscose rayon are made from treated plant cellulose, the threads of which are then twisted together to form a yarn. It is expensive to produce, easy-care, difficult to shrink, and resistant to moths and mould. It has a soft silky feel and drapes well and so is often used to imitate silk for fabrics such as brocade and moiré.

Synthetic Fibres

These are completely chemically derived. They were first developed as a cheaper substitute for natural fibres but the huge range now available offers a large choice in price and quality.

Acrylic has the bulky feel of wool and is warm, light and soft. It is strong and crease-resistant but picks up dirt easily. It is often mixed with wool and cotton. Dralon velvet is a particularly well-known form of acrylic pile fabric.

Nylon, the first synthetic fibre to be made, is strong, light and easy-care. It washes and dries quickly and does not crease, but white nylon discolours quickly. It can be made up into voile, lace, net, satin and seersucker; when waterproofed, it becomes ciré nylon, which is ideal for shower curtains.

Polyester can imitate wool, silk, cotton and linen. Hardwearing and crease-resistant, it is commonly blended with cotton for easy-care sheeting. Polyester net is not affected by strong sunlight.

FABRIC WEAVES

Weave is basically the interlacing of two sets of threads that cross each other at right angles. Lengthwise threads, known as *warp*, intersect the crosswise threads, called *weft*. There can be infinite variations on this theme. There are *plain weaves* (weft threads under and over warp threads) which produce fabrics such as muslin and gingham. Taffeta is a plain weave made from silk or silk-like fibres. *Twill* is created by the staggered interlacing of two warp and weft threads which form a diagonal pattern on each side of the cloth, to produce fabrics such as herringbone, ticking and tartan. Fabrics like damask contain more than one weave structure, creating a woven-in pattern. Brocade is a damask to which threads in gold or silver (or other colours) have been added.

SPECIAL FINISHES

There are various special finishes which give a fabric a certain look or texture. Chemical processes such as glazing employ a combination of friction, heat and pressure to give the cloth a light, luxurious sheen. Glazing also makes the fabric less flexible and therefore less versatile in its usage. Moiré, in which the watermark is applied to the fabric in a heat process, results in a fabric that looks grander and has more depth than the original but is much more delicate. Any contact with water will remove the watermark and cause staining. Even dry-cleaning will eventually fade the watermark. Fabric can also be hand-dyed or painted. Natural fibres are the most receptive, and it is a particularly good way to make the most of cheap cottons and tickings.

PATTERN

Pattern provides one of the most exciting elements in fabrics. Different styles and periods as well as moods and atmospheres can be evoked by the use of appropriate pattern. The size of pattern should be considered carefully against the size of a room and the existing furnishings. Before selecting a fabric consider how it will look in position. Large prints work well on a big expanse of flat fabric and need space around them to get the full effect. Small patterns are lost on a large surface and when seen from a distance tend to recede into a textured blur, so simple, bold pattern would be preferable for a large window.

A strong motif looks good on a flat, regular surface, while geometric patterns look unbalanced on forms that do not match their own proportions. Swirling patterns such as floral designs disguise form and contours. When a form is strong it should be allowed to speak for itself by using plain fabric, perhaps interestingly textured. A strong pattern could always be toned down by using a contrasting plain border, which would also help define the shape of the furnishing.

In fact, borders can transform an otherwise unexciting treatment and give definition but they must be an integral part of the finished look. Cord, piping, binding and braid are all suitable. Interesting effects can be achieved by using plain against pattern, a mixture of two different patterns, or contrasting textures and colours.

Glossary

FABRICS

ACRYLIC Soft, lightweight, man-made fibre, which is warm, strong and crease-resistant.

BROCADE Originally of silk but can be made in cotton, linen, wool or man-made fibre. It is usually woven in one or two colours, with the additional colours applied to the woven surface, which is what distinguishes it from damask. Heavier than damask, it is often woven in silver or gold thread. It is used for curtains and special upholstery.

BROCATELLE A type of silk strengthened with linen. It seldom uses more than two colours. It has a satin or twill figure on a plain or satin ground and is distinguished from damask by raised areas of pattern that are formed by a double warp. It does not drape well and in the 17th century was used mainly for wall hangings.

CALICO A cheap cotton of medium weight. It can also be printed, and fabric paints and stencils work well on it. It does shrink easily and looks best on tightly fitted upholstery.

CANVAS A plain basket-weave material of coarse jute threads. It is made in various weights and is the basic material from which buckram is made.

CHINTZ A plain or printed cotton with or without a glazed finish. It is not especially hard-wearing, and glazed chintzes in particular do not drape very well. It is best suited to curtains or small items of upholstery but can be strengthened with a lining backing. It suffers some shrinkage if washed. Antique chintz can be used in panels and as borders.

COTTON Available in a wide range of weights and finishes. The unmixed version creases easily but a cotton/synthetic mixture can be more practical. Furnishing cottons should always be used, as dressmaker's cotton is simply not strong enough.

CORDUROY Hard-wearing cloth usually of cotton but sometimes of synthetic yarns with a cotton backing-cloth. Equally spaced cords run down the length of the fabric and are obtainable in different widths.

CRETONNES A boldly printed cotton fabric available with glaze or twill, suitable for curtains and upholstered furniture. It is more hard-wearing than chintz.

CREWELWORK Originally hand-embroidered in chain, stem or herringbone stitch onto white cotton or wool in designs such as a tree of life or flowers and leaves and used for early English and American bed hangings. It is now available by the metre and is suitable for window and bed curtains, light upholstery and cushions.

DAMASK Was traditionally made from silk from Damascus but is distinguished by the weave rather than the fibre content and can also be made in silk, cotton, linen, wool or man-made fibres. Its durability depends on its fibre content, so it should be chosen accordingly. The patterns are fluid but formal. The formality of the pattern does not work well with modern interiors. It is mainly used in restoration work for upholstery and formal full-length curtains. Early damasks had huge pattern repeats suited to the tall windows to be curtained. The patterns show to advantage on a large flat area and so work particularly well when stretched on walls. Damask curtains are always heavy and need extra-strong fixings.

DUPION Originally made from an irregular thickness of silks, this medium-weight fabric can now be produced from various fibres. It has a slubbed appearance and comes in many colours. It is mainly used for curtains.

GAUFRAGE From the French word for embossing or stamping, a pattern is applied to a fabric by means of heated rollers. It is mostly done on velvet for upholstery.

GEORGETTE Available in many fibres and a fine fabric with a crepelike texture. It is available in a wide range of colours and drapes well. It can be used for lightweight curtains for beds and windows and for Austrian blinds.

GINGHAM A light, washable cotton fabric in a check pattern of two colours on white. It is often used in kitchens and children's rooms and for table linen.

HERRINGBONE A twill weave, usually wool or tweed, achieved by alternating the diagonal pattern within the cloth. It is suitable for upholstery.

INDIENNE A type of printed cotton first imported towards the end of the 16th century.

JACQUARD The name of the loom which originally had a series of punched cards to control the weaving of the threads; computerized versions are used today. The resulting patterns are usually multi-coloured and elaborate.

LINEN A strong cloth spun from flax. Its disadvantages are a tendency to shrink and crease. It is more practical when blended with cotton to form a linen union, and can also be strengthened with synthetic yarn. It is used for chair and sofa slip-covers and occasionally curtains, though it can be a little stiff to drape well.

MOIRÉ Sometimes called watered silk. It is finished with a process that gives the fabric a wavy effect. Used for light upholstery, walling and cushions.

OTTOMAN Available in cotton, silk and synthetic yarns, it has a horizontal rib pattern, the stripes of which can be in different colours. It is hardwearing and suitable for upholstery.

PLUSH A cut-pile fabric similar to velvet but with a longer, less dense pile.

REP A ribbed cloth of lightly woven cotton.

SATIN Can be made of silk, cotton or synthetic fibres. The surface is smooth and shiny and the reverse side matt. It is not the most practical fabric as it tends to spot easily and is difficult to clean.

SHANTUNG A plain woven fabric of silk or synthetic with a slubbed appearance, used for curtains and cushions.

SILK A natural fabric from silk worms. It dyes well and has a vibrant colour range. It fades easily in sunlight, however, and is best used on beds away from the light, or lined and interlined and protected by a blind if used as window curtains. It can be used for light, elegant upholstery. Until the early 16th century silks had large patterns and were made for specific purposes such as upholstery and wall coverings. The Jacquard loom produced figured silks, and the Industrial Revolution made mass production of silks possible by the mid 19th century.

SILK NOIL The waste product of spun silk is mixed with cotton or wool giving a shimmer to the fabric in the form of tiny balls on the surface.

TAFFETA Originally made of silk it can now be of any plain-woven fabric. It is smooth and crisp, sometimes ribbed, but not very pliable. It can be "shot" for a shimmering effect.

TAPESTRY Woven either by hand or by machine. The latter is sold by the metre (yard) as a Jacquard imitation. Available in a wide variety of designs and colours, it is used for chair upholstery and cushions.

THAI SILK An iridescent fabric, slubbed and dyed in vivid colours. It is very expensive.

TICKING A stiff fabric in twill weave originally developed for mattress and pillow covers. Cheap, hard-wearing and effective, it is good for Roman and roller blinds and upholstery on modern or traditional chairs.

TOILE Printed cotton fabric. The original copperplate printing was done in Ireland in mid 18th century, and the famous factory at Jouy began printing them some 20 years later. Depicting charming rural scenes or Classical designs, it is used for curtains, bed hangings, wall hangings and light upholstery.

TWEED Made with wool yarns, it comes in a variety of textures and colours. It can be used for curtains and upholstery.

VELOUR A fabric with a thick pile that lies in one direction, it is made of cotton, wool or synthetic fibres. It is good for heavy curtains or tablecloths.

VELVET A closely woven pile fabric of cotton or synthetic fibre, it comes in a variety of weights and colours. It is best used flat or smoothly draped. A plain velvet used for upholstery can quickly look shabby, as the pile is flattened, while a light-coloured velvet will show the dust. Figured velvets are the most practical. Velvet curtains are good for insulation and blackout but can have a deadening effect on the room. In general, velvets do not mix well with modern fabrics and interiors.

WORSTED A hard-wearing wool fabric with a smooth texture which is useful for upholstery.

Sheers and Lightweight Fabrics

LACE Very light open-work fabric made from cotton, viscose or nylon; pattern can be applied to mesh ground. It is used in windows for privacy, as bed drapes and as romantic-style bedcovers, cushion covers and dressing-table skirts. It is also available as edging and in frills.

MUSLIN Lightweight gauze made from cotton. Sheer and crisp, it can be patterned with floral motifs. It is inexpensive but tends to shrink and crease.

NET A very light, open-mesh, almost transparent fabric made from cotton, silk or man-made fibres, usually in white or cream but these days available in a wide range of colours including dramatic dark ones.

CHEESECLOTH A light, soft fabric slightly more densely woven than muslin.

POPLIN Light- to medium-weight cotton or rayon fabric which has a fine rib and slight sheen. It is inexpensive and drapes well. The heavier, ribbed fabric can even be used for loose covers.

VOILE A fine crisp fabric made from cotton, silk, wool or synthetic fibres, it is suitable for sheer curtains and dressing-table skirts.

Linings

COTTON SATEEN The most popular form of curtain lining. It is usually buff-coloured but white lining looks better if it is being used with fabric printed on a white ground. Coloured linings chosen to contrast or coordinate with the curtaining can also look attractive.

BUCKRAM A stiffened cotton used for pelmets and tie-backs.

BUMP A cotton-waste interlining used to add body and insulation.

DOMETTE An interlining with a padded weave.

INSULATED LININGS May rely on the weight and composition of the fibres they contain or may incorporate metal particles on the reverse to reflect heat back into the room. Examples: Milium (which is metal-backed) for insulation without weight, roclon (a heavy rubberized fabric now available in white) for blackout and insulation.

WADDING Padded interlining usually made from polyester.

Trimmings

BLOCK FRINGE A fringe trimming coloured with equal blocks of contrasting colour.

BULLION FRINGE A fringe trimming formed of twisted loops of rope, made in wool or silk and available in a variety of lengths and thicknesses.

CHOU Ornamental curtain detail consisting of a circular gathered piece of fabric designed to give the illusion of a curtain having been caught up. The name is derived from the French word for "cabbage".

GIMP Woven braid used to ornament curtains, bed and chairs. It can be very complex in design.

PICOT BRAID A woven cotton braid of various widths with a bobble edging.

ROSETTES A device for focusing attention on a particular area with a curtain arrangement. An attractive "finishing-off" motif for curtain headings, swags and tails, and tie-backs. Can be knife-pleated, choux or bow style.

GENERAL TERMS

À LA DUCHESSE A type of bed with a canopy suspended from the ceiling rather than supported by posts (also known as an angel bed).

APPLIQUÉ A form of decoration produced by superimposing one material on another. It may consist of figured patterns cut out and applied, or embroidered bands of patterns.

ARABESQUE Decoration characterized by symmetrical intertwining branches, leaves and other plant forms together with abstract curvilinear shapes.

ARCHITRAVE A wooden surround to a door or window frame; also the moulding around an arch.

AUSTRIAN BLIND A soft fabric blind that pulls up on vertical cords into swags and appears gently ruched at the base when let down.

BATTEN A thin piece of timber that slots into the base hem of a roller blind or Roman blind so that the fabric hangs straight and rigid. Also timber struts nailed vertically to the wall for fabric walling.

BAY WINDOW A single, double or triple window that projects from the wall of a building, leaving a corresponding recess as part of a room. The wall beneath the window carries down to the ground.

BOX PLEATS Flat, symmetrical pleats formed by folding the fabric to the back at each side of a pleat.

CAFÉ CURTAIN Curtains hung to cover the bottom part of a window. Usually kept closed, they originated in Vienna in the 19th century.

CAFÉ ROD A slim rod, normally of brass, used for cased or scallop-headed curtains.

CANOPY BED with canopy suspended over the head by cords attached to the ceiling (see *À la Duchesse.*)

CASED HEADINGS (or slot heading) A curtain heading consisting of a simple hemmed top through which a rod or narrow pole may be slotted.

CASEMENT WINDOW Window which opens from the side.

CLOAKPIN A brass disc, often ornamented with ormolu, used to hold back curtains either by draping them behind the disc or by winding them around it. It is attached to the wall by a turned stem.

CORDING SET Equipment for drawing curtains with a pull cord.

CORNICE A decorative moulding at the top of a wall, just below the ceiling. Also a pelmet-like construction above a curtain arrangement.

CORNICE POLE A curtain pole with rings, used for heavy curtains.

CORONA A crown or ring usually of metal, forming the main support of bed drapes, centrally mounted on the wall above the bed.

CURTAIN CORNICE Decorative board, often carved, painted or gilded, placed above curtain heading or pelmet.

CURTAIN LINING Thin fabric, usually cotton, used to line curtains.

DADO Lower part of interior wall, beneath dado rail.

DADO-RAIL Moulding dividing lower part of wall (dado) from upper (infill). Originally designed to stop chair backs from damaging wall decoration, it is known as a chair rail in the United States.

DEADLIGHT Space immediately above the window architrave and below the ceiling and cornice.

DORMER WINDOW Window in a sloping roof, with vertical sides and front.

DOUBLE-HUNG WINDOW See Sash window.

DRAW ROD Rod inserted into the heading used to open and close curtains.

DRESS CURTAIN Curtain that does not close but is hung for effect.

FAUX FINISHES Decorative paint finishes to represent marble, wood-graining, stone etc.

FESTOON Curtain fixed at the top and drawn up in one piece on vertical cords to form a swag. Also refers to decoration representing a garland tied together with ribbons and suspended between two points so that it drapes in the middle. Widely used in classical ornamentation, it is also known as a swag.

FIGURED WEAVE Patterned by the weave structure, as in figured silks or velvets.

FINIAL Decorative end of a curtain pole which also prevents rings and curtains from sliding off.

FITTED BEDCOVER Cover with flat top panel, box strip corresponding to depth of mattress and skirt which can be straight with inverted pleats at each corner, box pleated or gathered.

FOUR-POSTER Bed framework supporting a valanced ceiling and four curtains. There have been many possible variations on the theme. Also called full tester.

FRENCH PLEATS Hand-sewn triple pleats separated by flat areas on a curtain heading. Also called pinch pleats.

FULL TESTER See Four-poster.

GLAZING BARS The bars of wood or metal which hold panes of glass in place.

GOBLET HEADING A curtain heading consisting of hand-sewn "goblet"-shaped tubes whose tops are stuffed with wadding or contrasting fabric.

GROTESQUE Ornamental motif based on Roman ornament found in grotto (underground chamber) of Golden House of Nero, featuring coiling foliage with people and animals and arabesques.

HALF-TESTER A rectangular canopy above a bed, extending only part-way down the bed from the headboard. The curtain draped at either side created a shallow three-dimensional effect.

HEADING Top edge of a curtain from which the curtain is hung.

HEADING TAPE Gathering tape purpose-made to give various heading styles.

HOLD-BACKS Decorative kinds of wood or metal fixed to the wall on either side of a window. Curtains are looped over them when drawn open.

INTERLINING A soft material sewn between a curtain and its lining to add bulk to improve the "hang" of the curtain and its insulation.

INVERTED PLEAT A pleat formed like a box pleat in reverse, so that the edges of the pleat meet in the middle on the right side of the fabric.

ITALIAN STRINGING A way of drawing curtains in which the curtains are joined in the centre and the actual heading remains fixed while the curtains draw backwards and forwards by means of diagonally strung cords placed about one-third of the way down the curtains; also called reefed curtains.

KNIFE PLEATS Sharply pressed, narrow, closely spaced pleats all running in the same direction.

JARDINIÈRE CURTAINS Usually sheer, with the bottom of the curtain rising in the centre to give a curved finish and reveal some of the window.

LAMBREQUIN Stiff, shaped pelmet inspired by the elaborate harnesses of horses. They were first used in 17th century French interiors often in conjunction with portières. As they developed over the centuries, they frequently continued down the sides of the frame to form a surround to the window.

LINING A secondary hanging sewn in at the back of a curtain to protect it from the light and improve its hanging qualities.

MULLIONS Vertical bars of stone or wood dividing the lights of a window.

ORMOLU Pale yellow gilt or bronzed metallic ware normally covered with a protective coat of clear lacquer.

PALLADIAN WINDOW A window with a high, round-topped central section and two lower, square-topped side sections. Also called Venetian window.

PASSEMENTERIE Trimmings used on curtains, blinds, pelmets, bed hangings and cushions to give definition and add decorative detail.

PELMET BOARD A horizontal board used to support a pelmet and sometimes as a base for swags and tails.

PENCIL-PLEAT HEADING A curtain formed by a tape which, when drawn up, creates a row of narrow, densely packed folds.

PIANO NOBILE The principal floor of a large house, with higher ceilings than the ground floor/basement or floor(s) above, and containing the main reception rooms. Based on Italian Renaissance ideas, and meaning "noble floor".

PINCH PLEATS See French pleats.

PINOLEUMS Very narrow wooden slatted blinds.

PORTIÈRE Curtain that hangs behind a door to cover it completely and keep out draughts.

POLONAISE A bed set lengthwise against the wall, sometimes in an alcove, surmounted by a small dome and elaborately dressed. Usually has high ends. Also refers to style of 18th century dress.

PRE-CORDED TRACK Curtain track bought with an integral cording system for closing and opening curtains.

PULL-UPS Curtains which pull up vertically (can be festoon, Austrian or other).

RECESS The window niche in which a window is fitted.

RECESSED FITTING Curtain or blind fixed within the recess of a window.

REEFED CURTAINS See Italian stringing.

RETURN The part of a curtain, pelmet or valance that turns around the sides of a window.

REVEAL Side wall of window niche.

ROCAILLE Ornamental style of 18th century with stylized pebbles, shell shapes and scrolls typical of Rococo decoration.

ROLLER BLIND A corded blind with horizontally set rods at the back causing the blind to form a series of lateral pleats when raised.

SASHES Fabric stretched over wooden frame and placed over lower half of window in 17th century to keep out sunlight and give privacy.

SASH WINDOW Window which slides open vertically. Also known as Double-hung window.

SCALLOPED HEADING A heading with deep, rounded cut-outs, which slots onto a rod or pole.

SCARF DRAPERY Uncut fabric draped to form an ornamental drapery.

SLIP-COVER Protective covering made in inexpensive fabric to protect expensive upholstery such as silk.

SLOT HEADING See Cased heading.

SMOCKED HEADING A heading of pencil pleats anchored together at regular intervals to create a honeycomb effect.

STORE MARQUISE 18th century French blind in lightweight material tightly gathered – now a general term for a shirred window panel.

STRAPWORK An ornamentation of crossed, interlaced and scrolled straps resembling leather often used to decorate walls in the 17th century.

SWAG A generous swoop of fabric hanging from two fixed points over a window or bed. Also known as a festoon.

SWAGS AND TAILS A decorative pleated arrangement of fabric hung at the top of curtains to hide the track. Swags are draped horizontally while tails hang on either side of the curtain.

TAILS Hanging trail of fabric, either shaped and stiffened or falling fluidly from the end of swags.

TAPE-GATHERED HEADING A curtain heading framed by a narrow, threaded tape sewn on at the top of a curtain. When the parallel threads are pulled up, a gathered effect is created.

TENTED CEILING A ceiling covered in fabric to imitate the inside of a tent.

TROMPE L'OEIL Images to "trick the eye" and give an illusion of reality.

TRUNDLE OR TRUCKLE BEDS 17th century beds on wheels which could be stowed away.

TURKEY WORK Use of knotted work to imitate effect of Oriental rugs.

VALANCE Soft-style curtain pelmet, pelmet around bed tester or skirt around base of bed.

VENETIAN WINDOW See Palladian window.

ACKNOWLEDGEMENTS

Reproduced by courtesy of the American Museum in Britain, Bath, pp32, 58; Peter Aprahamian pp2, 28, 46, 112, 130, 187, 200; Arcaid/Ken Kirkwood p161; from *Art Deco Designs*, Bracken Books, 1988, pp170, 179; Boys Syndication pp20, 83; Bridgeman Art Library pp8, 19, 22, 25, 102, 109, 128, 142, 147; British Library (Add Ms28962) p11; Albert E. Chapman Ltd., London, pp138, 183, 210 left; Colefax and Fowler pp89 right, 199, /Chester Jones p197; Crown Copyright, Historic Royal Palaces pp35, 41; *Country Life* Magazine Photographic Library p207; Wendy A. Cushing Ltd., Unit M7, Chelsea Garden Market, Chelsea Harbour, London SW10 0XE, tel. 071-351 5796, pp66, 124; *Decorative Arts Studio Yearbook*, 1934, p166; *Decorative Arts Studio Yearbook*, 1953-4, Studio Publications, pp182, 186; Design Press, Stockholm pp106-7; Durley House Hotel, London, tel. 071-235 5537, p190; EWA pp44, 52, 55, 62, 63, 80-1, 91, 94, 135, 148, 192-3, 203, 208, 210 right, /Cassell pp73, 74, 88; from *Farbige Raumkunst, Moderner Kunstler*, 1929, pp156, 158, 160; Fine Art Interiors, pp2, 120, 205; Michael Freeman pp86, 122, 139, 140-1; Derek Frost Associates, London, p188; loaned by Gainsborough Silk Weaving Co. Ltd., Sudbury, Suffolk, p43; The Green Room, Framlingham, Suffolk pp30, 155, /Jane Lewis p196; from *Les Habitats Modernes et Leur Décoration*, 1927, Paris, pp167, 168, 173, 178; Mr. Mohamed Al Fayed, Chairman of Harrods Ltd., for his kind permission to reproduce images from Catalogues in the Company Archives, pp143, 163, 174, 176; Heals Archives Design Museum, London, pp145, 159, 175; Bruce Hemming p126; Angelo Hornak pp16, 17, 31, 49, 98, 103, 111; Ipswich Borough Council Museums and Galleries pp13, 33; Ken Kirkwood pp60, 64; Susan Llewellyn, London, p202; London Borough of Lambeth Archives Dept. p105; Mansell Collection pp15, 59, 90, 144, 146; McKinney Kidston, London, p209; Merrick and Day, Gainsborough, Lincs. p152; Millar and Harris, Crown Copyright Reserved, p164; © National Trust 1991/Andreas von Einseidel p29, /Eric Pelham p35, /John Bethell pp36, 68, /Oliver Benn p71; Osborne & Little plc pp18, 39, 116, 180, 189; loaned by the O'Shea Gallery, London, pp57, 61, 70, 89 left, 95, 113 bottom left and right, 117, 118 right, 119 left, 136 left and right, 151, 172 left and right; The Pelham Hotel, London, tel. 071-589 8288, p184; English (unknown) fragment – American Independence 1776, © 1785, Philadelphia Museum of Art: Gift of Mrs. William D. Frismuth, p84; from George Smith's *The Cabinet Maker and Upholsterer's Guide*, 1826, pp101, 113 top left, 118 left, 119 right; Sunway U.K. Limited. p195; Eric Thorburn p132; from *Wallpapers, 17th Century to the Present Day*, Studio Editions, 1990, pp76, 113 top right, 131; Watford Council p110; courtesy Winterthur Museum, Winterthur, Delaware, U.S.A. pp85, 115; Photo Woodmansterne p14. Front cover design by Melanie Payne, reprinted by kind permission of Mrs. Caroline Clarke.

Index

DATE DUE

6/5/00			
11/22/00			
APR 17 2006			